Coaching
Youth Softball

Contents

Coaching Youth Softball

Third Edition

American Sport Education Program

Human Kinetics

Library of Congress Cataloging-in-Publication Data
Coaching youth softball / American Sport Education Program--3rd ed.
    p. cm.
    ISBN 0-7360-3717-9
        1. Softball for children--Coaching.   2. Softball--Coaching.   I. American Sport Education
    Program.
    GV881.4.C6 C63   2001
    796.357'8--dc21   00-050031
ISBN: 0-7360-3717-9

Material in chapters 4 and 6 is reprinted, by permission, from YMCA of the USA, 1999, *Coaching YMCA Winners Baseball and Softball* (Champaign, IL: Human Kinetics).

Acquisitions Editor: Thomas Hanlon; **Games Consultant**: Rich Bakker; **Developmental Editor**: Leigh LaHood; **Assistant Editor**: Kim Thoren; **Copyeditor**: John Wentworth; **Proofreader**: Julie A. Marx; **Graphic Designer**: Fred Starbird; **Graphic Artist**: Sandra Meier; **Cover Designer**: Jack W. Davis; **Photographer (cover)**: Jed DeKalb; **Photographer (interior)**: Tom Roberts; **Art Manager**: Craig Newsom; **Illustrators**: Mic Greenberg, Sharon Smith, and Tom Roberts (Mac art); Roberto Sabas (line drawings); **Printer**: United Graphics

Copies of this book are available at special discounts for bulk purchase for sales promotions, premiums, fund-raising, or educational use. Special editions or book excerpts can also be created to specifications. For details, contact the Special Sales Manager at Human Kinetics.

Printed in the United States of America   10   9   8   7   6   5   4   3   2   1

Human Kinetics
Web site: www.humankinetics.com

United States: Human Kinetics
P.O. Box 5076, Champaign, IL 61825-5076
800-747-4457
e-mail: humank@hkusa.com

Canada: Human Kinetics
475 Devonshire Road Unit 100, Windsor, ON N8Y 2L5
800-465-7301 (in Canada only)
e-mail: hkcan@mnsi.net

Europe: Human Kinetics
Units C2/C3 Wira Business Park, West Park Ring Road, Leeds LS16 6EB, United Kingdom
+44 (0) 113 278 1708
e-mail: hk@hkeurope.com

Australia: Human Kinetics
57A Price Avenue, Lower Mitcham, South Australia 5062
08 8277 1555
e-mail: liahka@senet.com.au

New Zealand: Human Kinetics
P.O. Box 105-231, Auckland Central
09-309-1890
e-mail: hkp@ihug.co.nz

A Message From the Amateur Softball Association

As the national governing body for the sport of softball in the United States, the Amateur Softball Association (ASA) takes great pride in its mission of promoting and servicing amateur softball. The ASA also takes very seriously the responsibility of providing quality education to youth softball coaches. Since 1987, the ASA has offered one of the finest coaching education programs in all of youth sports with its Volunteer Improvement Program (VIP) coaching education program.

The ASA's coaching education program services coaches at all levels, from the first year coach to experienced veterans. Coaches learn about a variety of topics, including skill development and training techniques, thereby fostering a more positive and enjoyable experience for their players. The ASA also offers an excellent resource library of instructional videotapes, educational books and publications, and camps and clinics.

As part of the ASA's ongoing commitment to the education of youth softball coaches, we suggest that you read the American Sport Education Program's *Coaching Youth Softball*. This is another excellent resource to assist the grassroots softball coach.

For more information about the ASA's coaching education program and how to join the ASA, write to the following address or visit our website:

Amateur Softball Association
2801 N.E. 50th Street
Oklahoma City, OK 73111
405-424-5266
www.softball.org

We thank you for coaching youth softball, and we commend you for wanting to become a better coach.

Yours in softball,

Ron A. Radigonda
Executive Director
Amateur Softball Association

Welcome to Coaching!

Coaching young people is an exciting way to be involved in sport. But it isn't easy. Some coaches are overwhelmed by the responsibilities involved in helping athletes through their early sport experiences. And that's not surprising, because coaching youngsters requires more than bringing the bats and balls to the field and letting the team play. It involves preparing players physically and mentally to compete effectively, fairly, and safely in their sport, and providing them with a positive role model.

This book will help you meet the challenges *and* experience the many rewards of coaching young athletes. In this book you'll learn how to meet your responsibilities as a coach, to communicate well and provide for safety, to use a highly effective method—the games approach—to teach tactics and skills, and to apply strategies for coaching on game day. We also provide three sets of season plans to guide you throughout your season.

This book serves as a text for the American Sport Education Program's Coaching Youth Sport course. If you would like more information about this course or other ASEP courses and resources, please contact us at

ASEP
P.O. Box 5076
Champaign, IL 61825-5076
1-800-747-5698
www.asep.com

Key to Diagrams

P = Pitcher

C = Catcher

1B = First baseman

2B = Second baseman

3B = Third baseman

SS = Shortstop

LF = Left-fielder

CF = Center-fielder

RF = Short-fielder

R = Runner

——— = Path of ball hit

——▶ = Movement of player

- - -▶ = Path of ball thrown

〰▶ = Path of ball rolled on ground

B = Batter

C = Coach

AC = Assistant coach

chapter 1

Stepping Into Coaching

If you are like most youth league coaches, you have probably been recruited from the ranks of concerned parents, sport enthusiasts, or community volunteers. Like many rookie and veteran coaches, you probably have had little formal instruction on how to coach. But when the call went out for coaches to assist with the local youth softball program, you answered because you like children and enjoy softball, and perhaps because you wanted to be involved in a worthwhile community activity.

Your initial coaching assignment may be difficult. Like many volunteers, you may not know everything there is to know about softball or about how to work with children. *Coaching Youth Softball* will help you learn the basics of coaching softball effectively.

To start, let's take a look at what's involved in being a coach. What are your responsibilities? We'll also talk about how to handle the situation when your child is on the team you coach, and we'll examine five tools for being an effective coach.

Your Responsibilities As a Coach

As a softball coach, you'll be called upon to do the following:

1. **Provide a safe physical environment.** Playing softball holds an inherent risk, but as a coach you're responsible for regularly inspecting the practice and competition fields (see the checklists for field surface, outside playing area, and equipment in chapter 6).

2. **Communicate in a positive way.** You'll communicate not only with your players but also with parents, umpires, and administrators. Communicate in a way that is positive and that demonstrates you have the best interests of the players at heart. Chapter 2 will help you communicate effectively and positively.

3. **Teach the tactics and skills of softball.** We'll show you an innovative "games approach" to teaching and practicing the tactics and skills young athletes need to know—an approach that kids thoroughly enjoy. We ask you to help all players be the best they can be. In chapter 5 we'll show you how to teach softball skills, and in chapter 9 we'll provide season plans for 8- to 9-year-olds, 10- to 11-year-olds, and 12- to 14-year-olds, respectively. In chapter 8 we'll provide descriptions of all the skills you'll need to teach and help you detect and correct errors that players typically make.

4. **Teach the rules of softball.** We'll ask you to teach your players the rules of softball. You'll find the main rules in chapter 7.

5. **Direct players in competition.** This includes determining starting lineups and a substitution plan, relating appropriately to umpires and to opposing coaches and players, and making tactical decisions during games (see chapter 6). Remember that the focus is not on winning at all costs, but in coaching your kids to compete well, do their best, and strive to win within the rules.

6. **Help your players become fit and value fitness for a lifetime.** We want you to help your players be fit so they can play softball safely and successfully. We also want your players to learn to become fit on their own, understand the value of fitness, and enjoy training. Thus, we ask you not to make them do push-ups or run laps for punishment. Make it fun to get fit for softball, and make it fun to play softball so they'll stay fit for a lifetime.

These are your responsibilities as a coach. But coaching becomes even more complicated when your child is a player on the team you coach. If this is the case, you'll have to take into account your roles as both a coach and a parent and think about how those roles relate to each other.

Coaching Your Own Child

Many coaches are parents, but the two roles should not be confused. Unlike your role as a parent, as a coach you are responsible not only to yourself and your child but also to the organization, all the players on the team (including your child), and their parents. Because of this additional responsibility, your behavior on the softball field will be different from your behavior at home, and your son or daughter may not understand why.

For example, imagine the confusion of a young boy who is the center of his parents' attention at home but is barely noticed by his father/coach in the sport setting. Or consider the mixed signals received by a young girl whose softball skill is constantly evaluated by a mother/coach who otherwise rarely comments on her daughter's activities. You need to explain to your son or daughter your new responsibilities and how they will affect your relationship when coaching.

Take the following steps to avoid problems in coaching your child:

- Ask your child if he or she wants you to coach the team.
- Explain why you wish to be involved with the team.
- Discuss with your child how your interactions will change when you take on the role of coach at practices or games.
- Limit your coaching behavior to when you are in the coaching role.
- Avoid parenting during practice or game situations to keep your role clear in your child's mind.
- Reaffirm your love for your child, irrespective of his or her performance on the softball field.

Now let's look at some of the qualities that will help you become an effective coach.

Five Tools of an Effective Coach

Have you purchased the traditional coaching tools—things like whistles, coaching clothes, sport shoes, and a clipboard? They'll help you coach, but to be a successful coach you'll need five other tools that cannot be bought. These tools are available only through self-examination and hard work; they're easy to remember with the acronym COACH:

C – Comprehension
O – Outlook
A – Affection
C – Character
H – Humor

Comprehension

Comprehension of the rules, tactics, and skills of softball is required. You must understand the basic elements of the sport. To assist you in learning about the game, we describe rules, tactics, and skills in chapters 7 and 8. We also provide season plans in chapter 9.

To improve your comprehension of softball, take the following steps:

- Read the sport-specific section of this book in chapters 7, 8, and 9.
- Read other softball coaching books, including those available from the American Sport Education Program (ASEP).
- Contact youth softball organizations.
- Attend softball clinics.
- Talk with more experienced coaches.
- Observe local college, high school, and youth softball games.

In addition to having softball knowledge, you must implement proper training and safety methods so your players can participate with little risk of injury. Even then, injuries may occur. And more often than not, you'll be the first person responding to your players' injuries, so be sure you understand the basic emergency care procedures described in chapter 3. Also, read in that chapter how to handle more serious sport injury situations.

Outlook

This coaching tool refers to your perspective and goals—what you are seeking as a coach. The most common coaching objectives are to (a) have fun, (b) help players develop their physical, mental, and social skills, and (c) win. Thus your *outlook* involves the priorities you set, your planning, and your vision for the future.

While all coaches focus on competition, we want you to focus on *positive* competition, keeping the pursuit of victory in perspective by making decisions that first are in the best interests of the players and second will help to win the game.

So how do you know if your outlook and priorities are in order? Here's a little test for you:

Which situation would you be most proud of?

a. Knowing that each participant enjoyed playing softball.

b. Seeing that all players improved their softball skills.

c. Winning the league championship.

Which statement best reflects your thoughts about sport?

a. If it isn't fun, don't do it.

b. Everyone should learn something every day.

c. Sport isn't fun if you don't win.

How would you like your players to remember you?

a. As a coach who was fun to play for.

b. As a coach who provided a good base of fundamental skills.

c. As a coach who had a winning record.

Which would you most like to hear a parent of a player on your team say?

a. Mike really had a good time playing softball this year.

b. Nicole learned some important lessons playing softball this year.

c. Willie played on the first-place softball team this year.

Which of the following would be the most rewarding moment of your season?

a. Having your team not want to stop playing, even after practice is over.

b. Seeing one of your players finally master the skill of fielding a ground ball and throwing accurately to the right base.

c. Winning the league championship.

Look over your answers. If you most often selected "a" responses, then having fun is most important to you. A majority of "b" answers suggests that skill development is what attracts you to coaching. And if "c" was your most frequent response, winning is tops on your list of coaching priorities. If your priorities are in order, your players' well-being will take precedence over your team's win-loss record every time.

ASEP has a motto that will help you keep your outlook in line with the best interests of the kids on your team. It summarizes in four words all you need to remember when establishing your coaching priorities:

Athletes First, Winning Second

This motto recognizes that striving to win is an important, even vital, part of sports. But it emphatically states that no efforts in striving to win should be made at the expense of the athletes' well-being, development, and enjoyment.

Take the following actions to better define your outlook:

1. Determine your priorities for the season.
2. Prepare for situations that challenge your priorities.
3. Set goals for yourself and your players that are consistent with those priorities.
4. Plan how you and your players can best attain those goals.
5. Review your goals frequently to be sure that you are staying on track.

Affection

This is another vital tool you will want to have in your coaching kit: a genuine concern for the young people you coach. It involves having a love for kids, a desire to share with them your love and knowledge of softball, and the patience and understanding that allow each individual playing for you to grow from his or her involvement in sport.

You can demonstrate your affection and patience in many ways, including these:

- Make an effort to get to know each player on your team.
- Treat each player as an individual.
- Empathize with players trying to learn new and difficult skills.
- Treat players as you would like to be treated under similar circumstances.
- Be in control of your emotions.
- Show your enthusiasm for being involved with your team.
- Keep an upbeat and positive tone in all of your communications.

Character

The fact that you have decided to coach young softball players probably means that you think participation in sport is important. But whether or not that participation develops character in your players depends as much on you as it does on the sport itself. How can you build character in your players?

Having good character means modeling appropriate behaviors for sport and life. That means more than just saying the right things. What you say and what you do must match. There is no place in coaching for the "Do as I say, not as I do" philosophy. Challenge, support, encourage, and reward every youngster, and your players will be more likely to accept, even celebrate, their differences. Be in control before, during, and after all practices and contests. And don't be afraid to admit that you were wrong. No one is perfect!

Consider the following steps to being a good role model:

- Take stock of your strengths and weaknesses.
- Build on your strengths.
- Set goals for yourself to improve upon those areas you would not like to see copied.
- If you slip up, apologize to your team and to yourself. You'll do better next time.

Humor

Humor is an often-overlooked coaching tool. For our use it means having the ability to laugh at yourself and with your players during practices and contests. Nothing helps balance the tone of a serious skill-learning session like a chuckle or two. And a sense of humor puts in perspective the many mistakes your players will make. So don't get upset over each miscue or respond negatively to erring players. Allow your players and yourself to enjoy the ups, and don't dwell on the downs.

Here are some tips for injecting humor into your practices:

- Make practices fun by including a variety of activities.
- Keep all players involved in games and skill practices.
- Consider laughter by your players a sign of enjoyment, not of waning discipline.
- Smile!

Communicating As a Coach

In chapter 1 you learned about the tools needed to COACH: Comprehension, Outlook, Affection, Character, and Humor. These are essentials for effective coaching; without them, you'd have a difficult time getting started. But none of the tools will work if you don't know how to use them with your athletes—and this requires skillful communication. This chapter examines what communication is and how you can become a more effective communicator-coach.

What's Involved in Communication?

Coaches often mistakenly believe that communication involves only instructing players to do something, but verbal commands are only a small part of the communication process. More than half of what is communicated is nonverbal. So remember when you are coaching: Actions speak louder than words.

Communication in its simplest form involves two people: a sender and a receiver. The sender transmits the message verbally, through facial expressions, and possibly through body language. Once the message is sent, the receiver must assimilate it successfully. A receiver who fails to attend or listen will miss parts, if not all, of the message.

How Can I Send More Effective Messages?

Young athletes often have little understanding of the rules and skills of softball and probably even less confidence in playing it. So they need accurate, understandable, and supportive messages to help them along. That's why your verbal and nonverbal messages are so important.

Verbal Messages

"Sticks and stones may break my bones, but words will never hurt me," isn't true. Spoken words can have a strong and long-lasting effect. And coaches' words are particularly influential because youngsters place great importance on what coaches say. Perhaps you, like many former youth sport participants, have a difficult time remembering much of anything you were told by your elementary school teachers, but you can still recall several specific things your coaches at that level said to you. Such is the lasting effect of a coach's comments to a player.

Whether you are correcting misbehavior, teaching a player how to hit the ball, or praising a player for good effort, you should consider a number of things when sending a message verbally. They include the following:

- Be positive and honest.
- State it clearly and simply.
- Say it loud enough, and say it again.
- Be consistent.

Be Positive and Honest

Nothing turns people off like hearing someone nag all the time, and athletes react similarly to a coach who gripes constantly. Kids particularly need encouragement because they often doubt their ability to perform in a sport. So look for and tell your players what they did well.

But don't cover up poor or incorrect play with rosy words of praise. Kids know all too well when they've erred, and no cheerfully expressed cliché can undo their mistakes. If you fail to acknowledge players' errors, your athletes will think you are a phony.

A good way to correct a performance error is to first point out what the athlete did correctly. Then explain in a positive way what he or she is doing wrong and show him or her how to correct it. Finish by encouraging the athlete and emphasizing the correct performance.

Be sure not to follow a positive statement with the word *but*. For example, don't say, "Way to watch the ball into your glove, Sarah. But when you throw to first, be sure to push off your back leg so you can get a little more zip on the ball." Saying it this way causes many kids to ignore the positive statement and focus on the negative one. Instead, say something like, "Way to watch the ball into your glove, Sarah. And if you push off on your back leg, you'll get a little more zip on your throw to first. OK, let's go."

State It Clearly and Simply

Positive and honest messages are good, but only if expressed directly in words your players understand. "Beating around the bush" is ineffective and inefficient. And if you do ramble, your players will miss the point of your message and probably lose interest. Here are some tips for saying things clearly:

- Organize your thoughts before speaking to your athletes.
- Explain things thoroughly, but don't bore them with long-winded monologues.
- Use language your players can understand. However, avoid trying to be hip by using their age group's slang vocabulary.

Say It Loud Enough, and Say It Again

Talk to your team in a voice that all members can hear and interpret. A crisp, vigorous voice commands attention and respect; garbled and weak speech is tuned out. It's OK, in fact, appropriate, to soften your voice when speaking to a player individually about a personal problem. But most of the time your messages will be for all your players to hear, so make sure they can! An enthusiastic voice also motivates players and tells them you enjoy being their coach. A word of caution, however: Don't dominate the setting with a booming voice that distracts attention from players' performances.

Sometimes what you say, even if stated loudly and clearly, won't sink in the first time. This may be particularly true when young athletes hear words they don't understand. To avoid boring repetition and yet still get your message across, say the same thing in a slightly different way. For instance, when an opposing baserunner is on first base, you might first tell your players, "OK, let's get the lead runner!" If they don't appear to understand, you might say, "On a ground ball, throw to second base for the force-out. Don't allow the runner to get to second base!" The second form of the message may get through to players who missed it the first time around.

Be Consistent

People often say things in ways that imply a different message. For example, a touch of sarcasm added to the words "Way to go!" sends an entirely different message than the words themselves suggest. Avoid sending such mixed messages. Keep the tone of your voice consistent with the words you use. And don't say something one day and contradict it the next; players will get their wires crossed.

Nonverbal Messages

Just as you should be consistent in the tone of voice and words you use, you should also keep your verbal and nonverbal messages consistent. An extreme example of failing to do this would be shaking your head, indicating disapproval, while at the same time telling a player, "Nice try." Which is the player to believe, your gesture or your words?

Messages can be sent nonverbally in a number of ways. Facial expressions and body language are just two of the more obvious forms of nonverbal signals that can help you when you coach.

Facial Expressions

The look on a person's face is the quickest clue to what he or she thinks or feels. Your players know this, so they will study your face, looking for any sign that will tell them more than the words you say. Don't try to fool them by putting on a happy or blank "mask." They'll see through it, and you'll lose credibility.

Serious, stone-faced expressions are no help to kids who need cues as to how they are performing. They will just assume you're unhappy or disinterested. Don't be afraid to smile. A smile from a coach can give a great boost to an unsure athlete. Plus, a smile lets your players know that you are happy coaching them. But don't overdo it, or your players won't be able to tell when you are genuinely pleased by something they've done or when you are just putting on a smiling face.

Body Language

What would your players think you were feeling if you came to practice slouched over, with your head down and shoulders slumped? Tired? Bored? Unhappy? What would they think you were feeling if you watched them during a contest with your hands on your hips, your jaws clenched, and your face reddened? Upset with them? Disgusted with an umpire? Mad at a fan? Probably some or all of these things would enter your players' minds. And none of these impressions is the kind you want your players to have of you. That's why you should carry yourself in a pleasant, confident, and vigorous manner. Such a posture not only projects happiness with your coaching role but also provides a good example for your young players, who may model your behavior.

Physical contact can also be a very important use of body language. A handshake, a pat on the head, an arm around the shoulder, or even a big hug are effective ways of showing approval, concern, affection, and joy to your players. Youngsters are especially in need of this type of nonverbal message. Keep within the obvious moral and legal limits, of course, but don't be reluctant to touch your players, sending a message that can only truly be expressed in that way.

How Can I Improve My Receiving Skills?

Now, let's examine the other half of the communication process—receiving messages. Too often very good senders are very poor receivers of messages. But as a coach of young athletes, you must be able to fulfill both roles effectively.

The requirements for receiving messages are quite simple, but receiving skills are perhaps less satisfying and therefore underdeveloped compared to sending skills. People seem to naturally enjoy hearing themselves talk more than hearing others talk. But if you read about the keys to receiving messages and make a strong effort to use them with your players, you'll be surprised by what you've been missing.

Attention!

First, you must pay attention; you must want to hear what others have to communicate to you. That's not always easy when you're busy coaching and have many things competing for your attention. But in one-on-one or team meetings with players, you must really focus on what they are telling you, both verbally and nonverbally. You'll be amazed at the little signals you pick up. Not only will such focused attention help you catch every word your players say, but also you'll notice your players' moods and physical states. In addition, you'll get an idea of your players' feelings toward you and other players on the team.

Listen CARE-FULLY

How we receive messages from others, perhaps more than anything else we do, demonstrates how much we care for the sender and what that person has to tell us. If you care little for your players or have little regard for what they have to say, it will show in how you attend and listen to them. Check yourself. Do you find your mind wandering to what you are going to do after practice while one of your players is talking to you? Do you frequently have to ask your players, "What did you say?" If so, you need to work on your receiving mechanics of attending and listening. But perhaps the most critical question you should ask yourself, if you find that you're missing the messages your players send, is this: Do I care?

Providing Feedback

So far we've discussed separately the sending and receiving of messages. But we all know that senders and receivers switch roles several times during an interaction. One person initiates a communication by sending a message to another person, who then receives the message. The receiver then switches roles and becomes the sender by responding to the person who sent the initial message. These verbal and nonverbal responses are called *feedback*.

Your players will be looking to you for feedback all the time. They will want to know how you think they are performing, what you think of their ideas, and whether their efforts please you. Obviously, you can respond in many different ways. How you respond will strongly affect your players. They will respond most favorably to positive feedback.

Praising players when they have performed or behaved well is an effective way of getting them to repeat (or try to repeat) that behavior in the future. And positive feedback for effort is an especially effective way to motivate youngsters to work on difficult skills. So rather than shouting and providing negative feedback to players who have made mistakes, try offering players positive feedback, letting them know what they did correctly and how they can improve.

Sometimes just the way you word feedback can make it more positive than negative. For example, instead of saying, "Don't throw the ball that way," you might say, "Throw the ball this way." Then your players will be focusing on what to do instead of what not to do.

You can give positive feedback verbally and nonverbally. Telling a player, especially in front of teammates, that he or she has performed well is a great way to boost the confidence of a youngster. And a pat on the back or a handshake can be a very tangible way of communicating your recognition of a player's performance.

Who Else Do I Need to Communicate With?

Coaching involves not only sending and receiving messages and providing proper feedback to players but also interacting with parents, fans, game officials, and opposing coaches. If you don't communicate effectively with these groups of people, your coaching career will be unpleasant and short-lived. So try the following suggestions for communicating with these groups.

Parents

A player's parents need to be assured that their son or daughter is under the direction of a coach who is both knowledgeable about the sport and concerned about the youngster's well-being. You can put their worries to rest by holding a preseason parent-orientation meeting in which you describe your background and your approach to coaching.

If parents contact you with a concern during the season, listen to them closely and try to offer positive responses. If you need to communicate with parents, catch them after a practice, give them a phone call, or send a note through the mail. Messages sent to parents through players are too often lost, misinterpreted, or forgotten.

Fans

The stands probably won't be overflowing at your contests, but that only means that you'll more easily hear the few fans who criticize your coaching. When you hear something negative said about the job you're doing, don't respond. Keep calm, consider whether the message had any value, and if not, forget it. Acknowledging critical, unwarranted comments from a fan during a contest will only encourage others to voice their opinions. So put away your "rabbit ears" and communicate to fans, through your actions, that you are a confident, competent coach.

Prepare your players for fans' criticisms. Tell them it is you, not the spectators, they should listen to. If you notice that one of your players is rattled by a fan's comment, reassure the player that your evaluation is more objective and favorable—and the one that counts.

Umpires

How you communicate with umpires will have a great influence on the way your players behave toward them. Therefore, you need to set an example. Greet umpires with a handshake, an introduction, and perhaps some casual conversation about the upcoming contest. Indicate your respect for them before, during, and after the contest. Don't make nasty remarks, shout, or use disrespectful body gestures. Your players will see you do it, and they'll get the idea that such behavior is appropriate. Plus, if the umpire hears or sees you, the communication between the two of you will break down.

Opposing Coaches

Make an effort to visit with the coach of the opposing team before the game. During the game, don't get into a personal feud with the opposing coach. Remember, it's the kids, not the coaches, who are competing. And by getting along well with the opposing coach, you'll show your players that competition involves cooperation.

chapter 3

Providing for Players' Safety

One of your players rounds third, heading for home. She makes a hard slide into the plate as the catcher tags her. The umpire rules "safe," but you stop cheering when you notice that your player is unable to get on her feet and seems to be in pain. What do you do?

No coach wants to see players get hurt. But injury remains a reality of sport participation; consequently, you must be prepared to provide first aid when injuries occur and to protect yourself against unjustified lawsuits. Fortunately, there are many preventive measures coaches can institute to reduce the risk. In this chapter we describe

- steps you can take to prevent injuries,
- first aid and emergency responses for when injuries occur, and
- your legal responsibilities as a coach.

The Game Plan for Safety

You can't prevent all injuries from happening, but you can take preventive measures that give your players the best possible chance for injury-free participation. In creating the safest possible environment for your athletes, we'll explore what you can do in these six areas:

- Preseason physical examinations
- Physical conditioning
- Equipment and facilities inspection
- Player match-ups and inherent risks
- Proper supervision and record keeping
- Environmental conditions

We'll begin with what should take place *before* the season begins: the preseason physical examination.

Preseason Physical Examination

We recommend that your players have a physical examination before participating in softball. The exam should address the most likely areas of medical concern and identify youngsters at high risk. We also suggest that you have players' parents or guardians sign a participation agreement form and a release form to allow their children to be treated in case of an emergency.

Physical Conditioning

Players need to be in, or get in, shape to play the game at the level expected. To do so, they'll need to have adequate *cardiorespiratory fitness* and *muscular fitness*.

Cardiorespiratory fitness involves the body's ability to store and use oxygen and fuels efficiently to power muscle contractions. As players get in better shape, their bodies are able to more efficiently deliver oxygen and fuels to muscles and carry off carbon dioxides and other wastes. At times, softball involves lots of running; youngsters who aren't as fit as their peers often overextend in trying to make up for their lack of fitness, which could result in lightheadedness and nausea.

An advantage of teaching softball with the games approach is that kids are active during almost the entire practice; there is no standing around in lines, watching teammates take part in drills. Players will be attaining higher levels of cardiorespiratory fitness as the season progresses simply by taking part in practice. However, watch closely for signs of low levels of cardiorespiratory fitness; don't let your athletes do too much until they're fit. You might privately counsel youngsters who appear overly winded, suggesting that they train outside of practice to increase their fitness.

Muscular fitness encompasses strength, muscle endurance, power, speed, and flexibility. This type of fitness is affected by physical maturity, as well as strength training and other types of training. Your players will likely exhibit a relatively wide range of muscular fitness. Those who have greater muscular fitness will be able to run faster and throw harder. They will also sustain fewer muscular injuries, and any injuries that do occur will tend to be more minor in nature. And in case of injury, recovery rate is accelerated in those with higher levels of muscular fitness.

Two other components of fitness and injury prevention are the warm-up and the cool-down. Although young bodies are generally very limber, they, too, can get tight from inactivity. The warm-up should address each muscle group and get the heart rate elevated in preparation for strenuous activity. Have players warm up for 5 to 10 minutes by playing easy games and stretching.

As practice winds down, slow players' heart rates with an easy jog or walk. Then have players stretch for five minutes to help avoid stiff muscles and make them less tight before the next practice or contest.

Equipment and Facilities Inspection

Another way to prevent injuries is to ensure that all players wear approved helmets when hitting, preparing to hit in the on-deck circle, and running the bases.

Remember also to examine regularly the field on which your players practice and play. Remove hazards, report conditions you cannot remedy, and request maintenance as necessary. If unsafe conditions exist, either make adaptations to avoid risk to your players' safety or stop the practice or game until safe conditions have been restored.

Player Match-Ups and Inherent Risks

We recommend you group teams in two-year age ranges if possible. You'll encounter fewer mismatches in physical maturation with narrow age ranges. Even so, two 12-year-old girls might differ by 60 pounds in weight, a foot in height, and three or four years in emotional and intellectual maturity. This presents dangers for the less mature. Whenever possible, match players against opponents of similar size and physical maturity. Such an approach gives smaller, less mature youngsters a better chance to succeed and avoid injury while providing more mature players with a greater challenge. Closely supervise games so that the more mature do not put the less mature at undue risk.

Proper matching helps protect you from certain liability concerns. But you must also warn players of the inherent risks involved in playing softball, because "failure to warn" is one of the most successful arguments in lawsuits against coaches. So, thoroughly explain the inherent risks of softball, and make sure each player knows, understands, and appreciates those risks.

The preseason parent-orientation meeting is a good opportunity to explain the risks of the sport to both parents and players. It is also a good occasion on which to have both the players and their parents sign waivers releasing you from liability should an injury occur. Such waivers do not relieve you of responsibility for your players' well-being, but they are recommended by lawyers.

Proper Supervision and Record Keeping

To ensure players' safety, you will need to provide both general supervision and specific supervision. *General supervision* is being in the area of activity so that you can see and hear what is happening. You should be

- immediately accessible to the activity and able to oversee the entire activity,
- alert to conditions that may be dangerous to players and ready to take action to protect them, and
- able to react immediately and appropriately to emergencies.

Specific supervision is direct supervision of an activity at practice. For example, you should provide specific supervision when you teach new skills and continue it until your athletes understand the requirements of the activity, the risks involved, and their own ability to perform in light of these risks. You need to also provide specific supervision when you notice either players breaking rules or a change in the condition of your athletes.

As a general rule, the more dangerous the activity, the more specific the supervision required. This suggests that more specific supervision is required with younger and less-experienced athletes.

As part of your supervision duty, you are expected to foresee potentially dangerous situations and to be positioned to help prevent them from occurring. This requires that you know softball well, especially the rules that are intended to provide for safety. Prohibit dangerous horseplay, and hold practices only under safe weather conditions. These specific supervisory activities, applied consistently, will make the play environment safer for your players and will help protect you from liability if a mishap does occur.

For further protection, keep records of your season plans, practice plans, and players' injuries. Season and practice plans come in handy when you need evidence that players have been taught certain skills, whereas accurate, detailed injury report forms offer protection against unfounded lawsuits. Ask for these forms from your sponsoring organization (appendix A has a sample injury report form), and hold onto these records for several years so that an "old softball injury" of a former player doesn't come back to haunt you.

Environmental Conditions

Most problems due to environmental factors are related to excessive heat or cold, though you should also consider other environmental factors such as severe weather and pollution. A little thought about the potential problems and a little effort to ensure adequate protection for your athletes will prevent most serious emergencies that are related to environmental conditions.

Heat

On hot, humid days the body has difficulty cooling itself. Because the air is already saturated with water vapor (humidity), sweat doesn't evaporate as easily. Therefore, body sweat is a less effective cooling agent, and the body retains extra heat. Hot, humid environments make athletes prone to heat exhaustion and heatstroke (see more on these in "Serious Injuries" on page 29). And if *you* think it's hot or humid, it's worse on the kids—not only because they're more active, but also because youngsters under the age of 12 have a more difficult time than adults regulating their body temperature. To provide for players' safety in hot or humid conditions, take the following preventive measures.

⊙ **Monitor weather conditions and adjust practices accordingly.** Figure 3.1 shows the specific air temperatures and humidity percentages that can be hazardous.

⊙ **Acclimatize players to exercising in high heat and humidity.** Athletes can make adjustments to high heat and humidity over 7 to 10 days. During this time, hold practices at low to moderate activity levels and give the players water breaks every 20 minutes.

⊙ **Switch to light clothing.** Players should wear shorts and white T-shirts.

⊙ **Identify and monitor players who are prone to heat illness.** Players who are overweight, heavily muscled, or out of shape will be more prone to heat illness, as are athletes who work excessively hard or who have suffered heat illness before. Closely monitor these athletes and give them water breaks every 15 to 20 minutes.

⊙ **Make sure athletes replace water lost through sweat.** Encourage your players to drink one liter of water each day outside of practice and contest times, to drink eight ounces of water every 20 minutes during practice or competition, and to drink four to eight ounces of water 20 minutes before practice or competition.

⊙ **Replenish electrolytes lost through sweat.** Sodium (salt) and potassium are lost through sweat. The best way to replace these nutrients is by eating a normal diet that contains fresh fruits and vegetables. Bananas are a good source of potassium. The normal American diet contains plenty of salt, so players don't need to go overboard in salting their food to replace lost sodium.

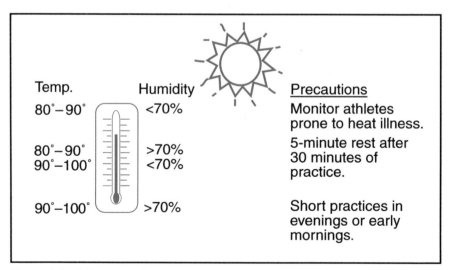

Temp.	Humidity	Precautions
80°–90°	<70%	Monitor athletes prone to heat illness.
80°–90° 90°–100°	>70% <70%	5-minute rest after 30 minutes of practice.
90°–100°	>70%	Short practices in evenings or early mornings.

Figure 3.1 Warm-weather precautions.

Water, Water Everywhere

Encourage players to drink plenty of water before, during, and after practice. Because water makes up 45 percent to 65 percent of a youngster's body weight and water weighs about a pound per pint, the loss of even a little bit of water can have severe consequences for the body's systems. And it doesn't have to be hot and humid for players to become dehydrated. Nor do players have to feel thirsty; in fact, by the time they are aware of their thirst, they are long overdue for a drink.

Cold

When a person is exposed to cold weather, the body temperature starts to drop below normal. To counteract this, the body shivers and reduces the blood flow to gain or conserve heat. But no matter how effective the body's natural heating mechanism is, the body will better withstand cold temperatures if it is prepared to handle them. To reduce the risk of cold-related illnesses, make sure players wear appropriate protective clothing, and keep them active to maintain body heat. Also monitor the windchill (see figure 3.2).

Severe Weather

Severe weather refers to a host of potential dangers, including lightning storms, tornadoes, hail, and heavy rains (which can cause injuries by creating sloppy field conditions).

	\multicolumn{9}{c}{Temperature (°F)}
Wind speed (mph)	0	5	10	15	20	25	30	35	40
40	-55	-45	-35	-30	-20	-15	-5	0	10
35	-50	-40	-35	-30	-20	-10	-5	5	10
30	-50	-40	-30	-25	-20	-10	0	5	10
25	-45	-35	-30	-20	-15	-5	0	10	15
20	-35	-30	-25	-15	-10	0	5	10	20
15	-30	-25	-20	-10	-5	0	10	15	25
10	-20	-15	-10	0	5	10	15	20	30
5	-5	0	5	10	15	20	25	30	35

Flesh may freeze within 1 minute

Windchill temperature (°F)

Figure 3.2   Windchill factor index.

Lightning is of special concern because it can come up quickly and can cause great harm or even kill. For each 5-second count from the flash of lightning to the bang of thunder, lightning is one mile away. A flash-bang of 10 seconds means lightning is two miles away; a flash-bang of 15 seconds indicates lightning is three miles away. A practice or competition should be stopped for the day if lightning is three miles away or less (15 seconds or less from flash to bang).

Safe places in which to take cover when lightning strikes are fully enclosed metal vehicles with the windows up, enclosed buildings, and low ground (under cover of bushes, if possible). It's *not* safe to be near metallic objects—flag poles, fences, light poles, metal bleachers, and so on. Also avoid trees, water, and open fields.

Cancel practice when under either a tornado watch or warning. If for some reason you are practicing or competing when a tornado is nearby, you should get inside a building if possible. If not, lie in a ditch or other low-lying area or crouch near a strong building, and use your arms to protect your head and neck.

The keys to handling severe weather are caution and prudence. Don't try to get that last 10 minutes of practice in if lightning is on the horizon. Don't continue to play in heavy rains. Many storms can strike both quickly and ferociously. Respect the weather and play it safe.

Air Pollution

Poor air quality and smog can present real dangers to your players. Both short- and long-term lung damage are possible from participating in unsafe air. While it's true that participating in clean air is not possible in many areas, restricting activity is recommended when the air-quality ratings are worse than moderate or when there is a smog alert. Your local health department or air-quality control board can inform you of the air-quality ratings for your area and when restricting activities is recommended.

Responding to Players' Injuries

No matter how good and thorough your prevention program is, injuries may occur. When injury does strike, chances are you will be the one in charge. The severity and nature of the injury will determine how actively involved you'll be in treating the injury. But regardless of how seriously a player is hurt, it is your responsibility to know what steps to take. So let's look at how you should prepare to provide basic emergency care to your injured athletes and take the appropriate action when an injury does occur.

Being Prepared

Being prepared to provide basic emergency care involves three steps: being trained in cardiopulmonary resuscitation (CPR) and first aid, having an appropriately stocked first aid kit on hand at practices and games, and having an emergency plan.

CPR and First Aid Training

We recommend that all coaches receive CPR and first aid training from a nationally recognized organization (the National Safety Council, the American Heart Association, the American Red Cross, or the American Sport Education Program). You should be certified based on a practical test and a written test of knowledge. CPR training should include pediatric and adult basic life support and obstructed airway procedures.

First Aid Kit

A well-stocked first aid kit should include the following:

- List of emergency phone numbers
- Change for a pay phone (or cell phone and batteries)
- Face shield (for rescue breathing and CPR)
- Bandage scissors
- Plastic bags for crushed ice
- 3-inch and 4-inch elastic wraps
- Triangular bandages
- Sterile gauze pads—3-inch and 4-inch squares
- Saline solution for eyes
- Contact lens case
- Mirror
- Penlight
- Tongue depressors
- Cotton swabs
- Butterfly strips
- Bandage strips—assorted sizes
- Alcohol or peroxide
- Antibacterial soap
- First aid cream or antibacterial ointment
- Petroleum jelly

- Tape adherent and tape remover
- 1-1/2-inch white athletic tape
- Prewrap
- Sterile gauze rolls
- Insect sting kit
- Safety pins
- 1/8-inch, 1/4-inch, and 1/2-inch foam rubber
- Disposable surgical gloves
- Thermometer

Emergency Plan

An emergency plan is the final step in preparing to take appropriate action for severe or serious injuries. The plan calls for three steps:

1. **Evaluate the injured player.** Your CPR and first aid training will guide you here.

2. **Call the appropriate medical personnel.** If possible, delegate the responsibility of seeking medical help to another calm and responsible adult who is on hand for all practices and games. Write out a list of emergency phone numbers and keep it with you at practices and games. Include the following phone numbers:

- Rescue unit
- Hospital
- Physician
- Police
- Fire department

Take each athlete's emergency information to every practice and game (see appendix B). This information includes the person to contact in case of an emergency, what types of medications the athlete is using, what types of drugs he or she is allergic to, and so on.

Give an emergency response card (see appendix C) to the contact person calling for emergency assistance. This provides the information the contact person needs to convey and will help keep the person calm, knowing that everything he or she needs to communicate is on the card. Also complete an injury report form (see appendix A) for any injury that occurs and keep it on file.

3. **Provide first aid.** If medical personnel are not on hand at the time of the injury, you should provide first aid care to the extent of your

qualifications. Again, while your CPR and first aid training will guide you here, the following are important guidelines:

- Do not move the injured athlete if the injury is to the head, neck, or back; if a large joint (ankle, knee, elbow, shoulder) is dislocated; or if the pelvis, a rib, or an arm or leg is fractured.
- Calm the injured athlete and keep others away from him or her as much as possible.
- Evaluate whether the athlete's breathing is stopped or irregular, and if necessary, clear the airway with your fingers.
- Administer artificial respiration if the athlete's breathing has stopped. Administer CPR if the athlete's circulation has stopped.
- Remain with the athlete until medical personnel arrive.

Emergency Steps

Your emergency plan should follow this sequence:

1. Check the athlete's level of consciousness.
2. Have a contact person call the appropriate medical personnel and the athlete's parents.
3. Send someone to wait for the rescue team and direct them to the injured athlete.
4. Assess the injury.
5. Administer first aid.
6. Assist emergency medical personnel in preparing the athlete for transportation to a medical facility.
7. Appoint someone to go with the athlete if the parents are not available. This person should be responsible, calm, and familiar with the athlete. Assistant coaches or parents are best for this job.
8. Complete an injury report form while the incident is fresh in your mind (see appendix A).

Taking Appropriate Action

Proper CPR and first aid training, a well-stocked first aid kit, and an emergency plan help prepare you to take appropriate action when an injury occurs. We spoke in the previous section about the importance of providing first aid *to the extent of your qualifications.* Don't "play doctor" with injuries; sort out minor injuries that you can treat from those for which you need to call for medical assistance.

Next we'll look at taking the appropriate action for minor injuries and more serious injuries.

Minor Injuries

Although no injury seems minor to the person experiencing it, most injuries are neither life-threatening nor severe enough to restrict participation. When such injuries occur, you can take an active role in their initial treatment.

Scrapes and Cuts. When one of your players has an open wound, the first thing you should do is put on a pair of disposable surgical gloves or some other effective blood barrier. Then follow these four steps:

1. *Stop the bleeding* by applying direct pressure with a clean dressing to the wound and elevating it. The player may be able to apply this pressure while you put on your gloves. Do not remove the dressing if it becomes soaked with blood. Instead, place an additional dressing on top of the one already in place. If bleeding continues, elevate the injured area above the heart and maintain pressure.

2. *Cleanse the wound* thoroughly once the bleeding is controlled. A good rinsing with a forceful stream of water, and perhaps light scrubbing with soap, will help prevent infection.

3. *Protect the wound* with sterile gauze or a bandage strip. If the player continues to participate, apply protective padding over the injured area.

4. *Remove and dispose of gloves* carefully to prevent you or anyone else from coming into contact with blood.

For bloody noses not associated with serious facial injury, have the athlete sit and lean slightly forward. Then pinch the player's nostrils shut. If the bleeding continues after several minutes, or if the athlete has a history of nosebleeds, seek medical assistance.

Treating Bloody Injuries

You shouldn't let a fear of acquired immune deficiency syndrome (AIDS) stop you from helping a player. You are only at risk if you allow contaminated blood to come in contact with an open wound, so the surgical disposable gloves that you wear will protect you from AIDS should one of your players carry this disease. Check with your director or your organization for more information about protecting yourself and your participants from AIDS.

Strains and Sprains. The physical demands of softball practices and games often result in injury to the muscles or tendons (strains) or to the ligaments (sprains). When your players suffer minor strains or sprains, immediately apply the PRICE method of injury care:

P – Protect the athlete and injured body part from further danger or trauma.

R – Rest the area to avoid further damage and foster healing.

I – Ice the area to reduce swelling and pain.

C – Compress the area by securing an ice bag in place with an elastic wrap.

E – Elevate the injury above heart level to keep the blood from pooling in the area.

Bumps and Bruises. Inevitably, softball players make contact with each other and with the ground. If the force applied to a body part at impact is great enough, a bump or bruise will result. Many players continue playing with such sore spots, but if the bump or bruise is large and painful, you should act appropriately. Use the PRICE method for injury care and monitor the injury. If swelling, discoloration, and pain have lessened, the player may resume participation with protective padding; if not, the player should be examined by a physician.

Be Safe When Sliding

You want your players to be safe—rather than out—when sliding into a base. Even more importantly, you want them to slide safely and not injure themselves. The majority of sliding injuries in softball are from head-first slides. Teach and encourage your players to do feet-first slides only.

Serious Injuries

Head, neck, and back injuries; fractures; and injuries that cause a player to lose consciousness are among a class of injuries that you cannot and should not try to treat yourself. In these cases you should follow the emergency plan outlined on pages 26-27. We do want to examine more closely your role, however, in preventing and handling two heat illnesses: heat exhaustion and heatstroke.

Heat Exhaustion. Heat exhaustion is a shocklike condition caused by dehydration and electrolyte depletion. Symptoms include headache, nausea, dizziness, chills, fatigue, and extreme thirst. Profuse sweating is a key sign of heat exhaustion. Other signs include pale, cool, and clammy skin; rapid, weak pulse; loss of coordination; and dilated pupils (see figure 3.3 for signs and symptoms of heat exhaustion).

A player suffering from heat exhaustion should rest in a cool, shaded area; drink cool water; and have ice applied to the neck, back, or abdomen to help cool the body. You may have to administer CPR if necessary or send for emergency medical assistance if the athlete doesn't recover or his or her condition worsens. Under no conditions should the athlete return to activity that day or before he or she regains all the weight lost through sweat. If the player had to see a physician, he or she shouldn't return to the team until he or she has a written release from the physician.

Heatstroke. Heatstroke is a life-threatening condition in which the body stops sweating and body temperature rises dangerously high. It occurs when dehydration causes a malfunction in the body's temperature con-

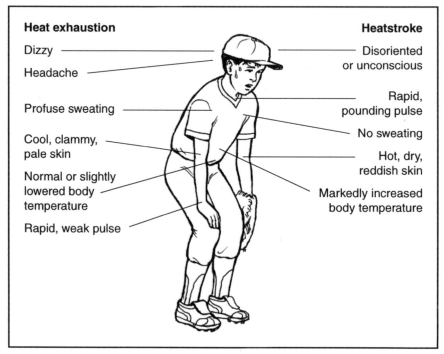

Figure 3.3 Signs and symptoms of heat exhaustion and heatstroke.

trol center in the brain. Symptoms include the feeling of being on fire (extremely hot), nausea, confusion, irritability, and fatigue. Signs include hot, dry, and flushed or red skin (this is a key sign); lack of sweat; rapid pulse; rapid breathing; constricted pupils; vomiting; diarrhea; and possibly seizures, unconsciousness, or respiratory or cardiac arrest. See figure 3.3 for signs and symptoms of heatstroke.

Send for emergency medical assistance immediately and have the player rest in a cool, shaded area. Remove excess clothing and equipment from the player, and cool the player's body with cool, wet towels or by pouring cool water over him or her. Apply ice packs to the armpits, neck, back, abdomen, and between the legs. If the player is conscious, have him or her drink cool water. If the player is unconscious, place the player on his or her side to allow fluids and vomit to drain from the mouth.

An athlete who has suffered heatstroke may not return to the team until he or she has a written release from a physician.

Protecting Yourself

When one of your players is injured, naturally your first concern is his or her well-being. Your feelings for youngsters, after all, are what made you decide to coach. Unfortunately, there is something else that you must consider: Can you be held liable for the injury?

From a legal standpoint, a coach has nine duties to fulfill. We've discussed all but planning in this chapter. (See chapter 5 for developing practice plans and chapter 9 for guidance on season planning.) The following is a summary of your legal duties:

1. Provide a safe environment.
2. Properly plan the activity.
3. Provide adequate and proper equipment.
4. Match, or equate, athletes.
5. Warn of inherent risks in the sport.
6. Supervise the activity closely.
7. Evaluate athletes for injury or incapacitation.
8. Know emergency procedures and first aid.
9. Keep adequate records.

Keep records of your season plan and practice plans and of players' injuries. Season and practice plans come in handy when you need evidence that players have been taught certain skills, and injury reports offer protection against unfounded lawsuits. Hold onto these records for several years so that an "old injury" of a former player doesn't come back to haunt you.

In addition to fulfilling these nine legal duties, you should check your organization's insurance coverage and your insurance coverage to make sure these policies will protect you from liability.

chapter 4

The Games Approach to Coaching Softball

Do you remember how as a kid you were taught by adults to play a sport, either in an organized sport program or physical education class? They probably taught you the basic skills using a series of drills that, if the truth be known, you found very boring. As you began to learn the basic skills, they eventually taught you the tactics of the game, showing you when to use these skills in various game situations. Do you remember how impatient you became during what seemed to be endless instruction, and how much you just wanted to play? Well, forget this traditional approach to teaching sport.

Now can you recall learning a sport by playing with a group of your friends in the neighborhood? You didn't learn the basic skills first; no time for that. You began playing immediately. If you didn't know the basic things to do, your friends told you quickly during the game so they could keep playing. Try to remember, because we're going to ask you to use a very similar approach to teaching softball to young people called the *games approach*, an approach we think knocks the socks off the traditional approach.

On the surface, it would seem to make sense to introduce softball by first teaching the basic skills of the sport and then the tactics of the game, but we've discovered that this approach has disadvantages. First, it teaches the skills of the sport out of the context of the game. Kids may learn to hit, field, and throw, but they find it difficult to use these skills in the real game. This is because they do not yet understand the fundamental tactics of softball and do not appreciate how best to use their newfound skills.

Second, learning skills by doing drills outside of the context of the game is so-o-o-o boring. The single biggest turnoff about adults teaching kids sport is that we overorganize the instruction and deprive kids of their intrinsic desire to play the game.

As a coach we're asking that you teach softball the games approach way. Clear the traditional approach out of your mind. Once you fully understand the games approach, you'll quickly see its superiority in teaching softball. Not only will kids learn the game better, but you and your players will have much more fun. And as a bonus, you'll have far fewer discipline problems.

With the games approach to teaching softball, we begin with a game. This will be a modified and much smaller game designed to suit the age and ability of the players. As the kids play in these "mini" games, you can begin to help them understand the nature of the game and to appreciate simple concepts of positioning and tactics. When your players understand what they must do in the game, they are then eager to develop the skills to play the game. Now that the players are motivated to learn the skills, you can demonstrate the skills of the game, practice using gamelike drills, and provide individual instruction by identifying players' errors and helping to correct them.

In the traditional approach to teaching sports, players do this:

Learn the skill → Learn the tactics → Play the game

In the games approach players do this:

Play the game → Learn the tactics → Learn the skill

In the past we have placed too much emphasis on the learning of skills and not enough on learning how to play skillfully—that is, how to use those skills in competition. The games approach, in contrast, emphasizes learning what to do first, then how to do it. Moreover—and this is a really important point—the games approach lets kids discover what to do in the game not by you telling them, but by their experiencing it. What you do as an effective coach is help them discover what they've experienced.

In contrast to the "skill-drill-kill the enthusiasm" approach, the games approach is a guided discovery method of teaching. It empowers your kids to solve the problems that arise in the game, and that's a big part of the fun in learning a game.

Now let's look more closely at the games approach to see the four-step process for teaching softball:

1. Play a modified softball game.
2. Help the players discover what they need to do to play the game successfully.
3. Teach the skills of the game.
4. Practice the skills in another game.

Step 1. Play a Modified Softball Game

Okay, it's the first day of practice; some of the kids are eager to get started, while others are obviously apprehensive. Some have rarely hit a ball, most don't know the rules, and few know the positions. What do you do?

If you use the traditional approach, you start with a little warm-up activity, then line the players up for a simple hitting drill and go from there. With the games approach, you begin by playing a modified game that is developmentally appropriate for the level of the players and also designed to focus on learning a specific part of the game.

Modifying the game means emphasizing a limited number of situations. This is one way you "guide" your players to discover certain tactics in the game. For instance, you set up an infield and place a runner on first base. The goal of the game for the defense is to prevent the runner from advancing to second base. Playing the game this way forces players to think about what they have to do to keep that runner from advancing.

Step 2. Help the Players Discover What They Need to Do

As your players are playing the game, look for the right spot to "freeze" the action, step in, and hold a brief question-and-answer session to discuss problems they were having in carrying out the goals of the game. You don't need to pop in on the first miscue, but if they repeat the same types of mental or physical mistakes a few times in a row, step in and ask them questions that relate to the aim of the game and the necessary skills required. The best time to interrupt the game is when you notice that they are having trouble carrying out the main goal, or aim, of the game. By stopping the game, freezing action, and asking questions, you'll help them understand

- what the aim of the game is,
- what they must do to achieve that aim, and
- what skills they must use to achieve that aim.

For example, your players are playing a game in which the objective is to keep the runner on first base from advancing to second base. You interrupt the game when you see they are having difficulties in achieving the aim and ask them the following questions:

Coach: What are you supposed to do in this game?

Players: Keep the runner from getting to second base safely.

Coach: What do you have to do to keep the runner from advancing?

Players: Force the runner at second.

Coach: Who covers the base if the ball is hit to the right side of the infield?

Players: The shortstop.

Coach: Who covers second if the ball is hit to the left side?

Players: The second-base player.

Coach: Let's practice making the force play at second base.

Through the modified game and skillful questioning on your part, your players realize that accurate fielding skills and tactical awareness are essential to their success in keeping runners from advancing. Just as important, rather than *telling* them that fielding skills and tactical awareness are critical, you led them to that discovery through a well-designed modified game and through questions. This questioning that leads to players' discovery is a crucial part of the games approach. Essentially you'll be asking your players—usually literally—"What do you need to do to succeed in this situation?"

Asking the right questions is a very important part of your teaching. At first asking questions will be difficult because your players have little or no experience with the game. And if you've learned sport through the traditional approach, you'll be tempted to tell your players how to play the game and not waste time asking them questions. Resist this powerful temptation to tell them what to do, and especially don't do so before they begin to play the game.

If your players have trouble understanding what to do, phrase your questions to let them choose between one option versus another. For example, if you ask them, "What's the best way to throw a runner out at third base from deep right field?" and get answers such as, "Throw it to the infield," or "Throw it to third base," then ask, "Should the right fielder throw all the way to third base or throw to the cutoff?"

Immediately following the question-and-answer session you will begin a skill practice, which is Step 3 of the four-step process.

Sometimes players simply need to have more time playing the game, or you may need to modify the game further so that it is even easier for them to discover what they are to do. It'll take more patience on your part, but it's a powerful way to learn.

Step 3. Teach the Skills of the Game

Only when your players recognize the skills they need to be successful in the game do you want to teach the specific skills through focused drills. This is when you use a more traditional approach to teaching sport skills, the "IDEA" approach, which we will describe in chapter 5.

Step 4. Practice the Skills in Another Game

Once the players have practiced the skill, you then put them in another game situation to let them practice the skill in the context of a game.

And that's the games approach. Your players will get to *play* more in practice, and once they learn how the skills fit into their performance and enjoyment of the game, they'll be more motivated to work on those skills, which will help them to be successful.

chapter 5

Teaching and Shaping Skills

Coaching softball is about teaching tactics, skills, fitness, and values. It's also about "coaching" players before, during, and after contests. Teaching and coaching are closely related, but there are important differences. In this chapter we'll focus on principles of teaching, especially on teaching softball skills. But many of the principles we'll discuss apply to teaching tactics, fitness concepts, and values as well. (Most of the other important teaching principles deal with communication, covered in chapter 2.) Then in chapter 6 we'll discuss the principles of coaching, which will guide your leadership activities before, during, and after contests.

Teaching Softball Skills

Many people believe that the only qualification needed to teach a skill is to have performed it. It's helpful to have performed it, but there is much more than that to teaching successfully. And even if you haven't performed the skill before, you can still learn to teach successfully with the useful acronym IDEA:

I – Introduce the skill.

D – Demonstrate the skill.

E – Explain the skill.

A – Attend to players practicing the skill.

These are the basic steps of good teaching. Now we'll explain each step in greater detail.

Introduce the Skill

Players, especially young and inexperienced ones, need to know what skill they are learning and why they are learning it. You should therefore take these three steps every time you introduce a skill to your players:

1. Get your players' attention.
2. Name the skill.
3. Explain the importance of the skill.

Get Your Players' Attention

Because youngsters are easily distracted, use some method to get their attention. Some coaches use interesting news items or stories. Others use jokes. And still others simply project enthusiasm to get their players to listen. Whatever method you use, speak slightly above the normal volume and look your players in the eye when you speak.

Also, position players so they can see and hear you. Arrange the players in two or three evenly spaced rows, facing you. (Make sure they aren't looking into the sun or at some distracting activity.) Then ask if everyone can see you before you begin.

Name the Skill

Although you might mention other common names for the skill, decide which one you'll use and stick with it. This will help avoid confusion and enhance communication among your players.

Explain the Importance of the Skill

Although the importance of a skill may be apparent to you, your players may be less able to see how the skill will help them become better softball players. Offer them a reason for learning the skill and describe how the skill relates to more advanced skills.

> The most difficult aspect of coaching is this: Coaches must learn to let athletes learn. Sport skills should be taught so they have meaning to the child, not just meaning to the coach.
>
> —Rainer Martens,
> founder of the American Sport Education Program

Demonstrate the Skill

The demonstration step is the most important part of teaching sport skills to players who may never have done anything closely resembling the skill. They need a picture, not just words. They need to see how the skill is performed.

If you are unable to perform the skill correctly, have an assistant coach, one of your players, or someone else more skilled perform the demonstration. These tips will help make your demonstrations more effective:

- Use correct form.
- Demonstrate the skill several times.
- Slow down the action, if possible, during one or two performances so players can see every movement involved in the skill.
- Perform the skill at different angles so your players can get a full perspective of it.
- Demonstrate the skill from both sides of the body.

Explain the Skill

Players learn more effectively when they're given a brief explanation of the skill along with the demonstration. Use simple terms and, if possible, relate the skill to previously learned skills. Ask your players whether they understand your description. A good technique is to ask the team to repeat your explanation. Ask questions like, "What are you going to do first?" and "Then what?" Watch for when players look confused or uncertain, and repeat your explanation and demonstration at those points. If possible, use different words so your players get a chance to try to understand the skill from a different perspective.

Complex skills often are better understood when they are explained in more manageable parts. For instance, if you want to teach your players how to field a ground ball and throw to first base, you might take the following steps:

1. Show them a correct performance of the entire skill, and explain its function in softball.

2. Break down the skill and point out its component parts to your players.

3. Have players perform each of the component skills you have already taught them, such as assuming the ready position and moving to the ball.

4. After players have demonstrated their ability to perform the separate parts of the skill in sequence, re-explain the entire skill.

5. Have players practice the skill in gamelike conditions.

One caution: Young players have short attention spans, and a long demonstration or explanation of the skill will bore them. So spend no more than a few minutes altogether on the introduction, demonstration, and explanation phases. Then get the players active in a game that calls on them to perform the skill. The total IDEA should be completed in 10 minutes or less, followed by games in which players practice the skill.

Attend to Players Practicing the Skill

If the skill you selected was within your players' capabilities and you have done an effective job of introducing, demonstrating, and explaining it, your players should be ready to attempt the skill. Some players may need to be physically guided through the movements during their first few attempts. Walking unsure athletes through the skill in this way will help them gain confidence to perform the skill on their own.

Your teaching duties don't end when all your athletes have demonstrated that they understand how to perform the skill. In fact, a significant part of your teaching will involve observing closely the hit-and-miss trial performances of your players. In the next section we'll guide you in shaping players' skills, and then we'll help you learn how to detect and correct errors using positive feedback. Keep in mind that your feedback will have a great influence on your players' motivation to practice and improve their performances.

Remember, too, that players need individual instruction. So set aside a time before, during, or after practice to give individual help.

Helping Players Improve Skills

After you have successfully taught your players the fundamentals of a skill, your focus will be on helping them improve that skill. Players will learn skills and improve upon them at different rates, so don't get too frustrated. Instead, help them improve by shaping their skills and detecting and correcting errors.

Shaping Players' Skills

One of your principal teaching duties is to reward positive behavior—in terms of successful skill execution—when you see it. A player makes a good hit in practice, and you immediately say, "That's the way to keep your head in there! Good swing!" This, plus a smile and a "thumbs-up" gesture, go a long way toward reinforcing that technique in that player.

Sometimes, however, you may have a long, dry spell before you have any correct technique to reinforce. It's difficult to reward players when they aren't executing skills correctly. How can you shape their skills if this is the case?

Shaping skills takes practice on your players' part and patience on your part. Expect your players to make errors. Telling the player who made the good hit that she did a good job doesn't ensure that she'll hit well the next time. Seeing inconsistency in your players' techniques can be frustrating. It's even more challenging to stay positive when your athletes repeatedly perform a skill incorrectly or lack enthusiasm for learning. It can certainly be frustrating to see athletes who seemingly don't heed your advice and continue to make the same mistakes. And when the athletes don't seem to care, you may wonder why you should.

Please know that it is normal to get frustrated at times when teaching skills. Nevertheless, part of successful coaching is controlling this frustration. Instead of getting upset, use these six guidelines for shaping skills:

1. **Think small initially.** Reward the first signs of behavior that approximate what you want. Then reward closer and closer approximations of the desired behavior. In short, use your reward power to shape the behavior you seek.

2. **Break skills into small steps.** For instance, in learning to field grounders and throw to a base, one of your players does well in getting into position and watching the ball into the glove, but he throws rather flat-footed to the base. Reinforce the correct techniques of getting into proper position and watching the ball into the glove, and teach him how to skip forward and prepare to throw. When he masters that, focus on getting him to complete the skill by pushing off the back leg after skipping forward and throwing the ball over the top.

3. **Develop one component of a skill at a time.** Don't try to shape two components of a skill at once. For example, in hitting, players must begin with a proper grip, get in a comfortable and appropriate stance, and use proper mechanics in the stride and swing. Players should focus first on one aspect at a time: grip, then stance, then stride, then swing. Athletes who have problems mastering a skill often do so because they're trying to improve two or more components at once. Help these athletes to isolate a single component.

4. **As athletes become more proficient at a skill, reinforce them only occasionally and only for the best examples of the skill behavior.** By focusing only on the best examples, you will help them continue to improve once they've mastered the basics.

5. **When athletes are trying to master a new skill, temporarily relax your standards for how you reward them.** As they focus on the new skill or attempt to integrate it with other skills, the old well-learned skills may temporarily degenerate.

6. **If, however, a well-learned skill degenerates for long, you may need to restore it by going back to the basics.**

Coaches often have more-skilled players provide feedback to teammates as they practice skills. This can be effective, but proceed with caution: You must tell the skilled players exactly what to look for when their teammates are performing the skills. You must also tell them the corrections for the common errors of that skill.

We've looked at how to guide your athletes as they learn skills. Now let's look at another critical teaching principle that you should employ as you're shaping skills: detecting and correcting errors.

Detecting and Correcting Errors

Good coaches recognize that athletes make two types of errors: learning errors and performance errors. *Learning errors* are ones that occur because athletes don't know how to perform a skill; that is, they have not yet developed the correct motor program in the brain to perform a particular skill. *Performance errors* are made not because athletes don't know how to do the skill, but because they made a mistake in executing what they do know. There is no easy way to know whether a player is making learning or performance errors. Part of the art of coaching is being able to sort out which type of error each mistake is.

The process of helping your athletes correct errors begins with your observing and evaluating their performances to determine if the mistakes are learning or performance errors. For performance errors, you need to look for the reasons that your athletes are not performing as well as they know how. If the mistakes are learning errors, then you need to help them learn the skill, which is the focus of this section.

There is no substitute for knowing skills well in correcting learning errors. The better you understand a skill—not only how it is done correctly but also what causes learning errors—the more helpful you will be in correcting mistakes.

One of the most common coaching mistakes is to provide inaccurate feedback and advice on how to correct errors. Don't rush into error correction; wrong feedback or poor advice will hurt the learning process more than no feedback or advice. If you are uncertain about the cause of the problem or how to correct it, continue to observe and analyze until you are more sure. As a rule, you should see the error repeated several times before attempting to correct it.

Correct One Error at a Time

Suppose Megan, one of your outfielders, is having trouble with her fielding. She tends to break in on the ball and often has to reverse direction while the ball goes over her head, and on the balls that she is in position to catch, she uses only one hand. What do you do?

First, decide which error to correct first, because athletes learn more effectively when they attempt to correct one error at a time. Determine whether one error is causing the other; if so, have the athlete correct that error first, because it may eliminate the other error. However, in Megan's case, neither error is causing the other. In such cases, athletes should correct the error that will bring the greatest improvement when remedied—for Megan, this would be getting back quickly on balls hit over her head. If balls are constantly going over her head, she needs to be positioned deeper. If they only occasionally go over her head, she needs to break her instinct of running toward the infield on every fly ball. Once she improves her ability to judge fly balls and get in proper position, then work on her catching the ball with two hands. Note that improvement in the first area may even motivate her to correct the other error.

Use Positive Feedback to Correct Errors

The positive approach to correcting errors includes emphasizing what to do instead of what not to do. Use compliments, praise, rewards, and encouragement to correct errors. Acknowledge correct performance as well as efforts to improve. By using the positive approach, you can help your athletes feel good about themselves and promote a strong desire to achieve.

When you're working with one athlete at a time, the positive approach to correcting errors includes four steps:

1. Praise effort and correct performance.
2. Give simple and precise feedback to correct errors.
3. Make sure the athlete understands your feedback.
4. Provide an environment that motivates the athlete to improve.

Let's take a brief look at each step.

Step 1: Praise Effort and Correct Performance. Praise your athlete for trying to perform a skill correctly and for performing any parts of it correctly. Praise the athlete immediately after he or she performs the skill, if possible. Keep the praise simple: "Good try," "Way to hustle," "Good form," or "That's the way to follow through." You can also use nonverbal feedback, such as smiling, clapping your hands, or any facial or body expression that shows approval.

Make sure you're sincere with your praise. Don't indicate that an athlete's effort was good when it wasn't. Usually an athlete knows when he or she has made a sincere effort to perform the skill correctly and perceives undeserved praise for what it is—untruthful feedback to make him or her feel good. Likewise, don't indicate that a player's performance was correct when it wasn't.

Step 2: Give Simple and Precise Feedback to Correct Errors. Don't burden a player with a long or detailed explanation of how to correct an error. Give just enough feedback so the player can correct one error at a time. Before giving feedback, recognize that some athletes will readily accept it immediately after the error; others will respond better if you slightly delay the correction.

For errors that are complicated to explain and difficult to correct, try the following:

⊙ Explain and demonstrate what the athlete should have done. Do not demonstrate what the athlete did wrong.

⊙ Explain the cause or causes of the error, if this isn't obvious.

⊙ Explain why you are recommending the correction you have selected, if it's not obvious.

Step 3: Make Sure the Athlete Understands Your Feedback. If the athlete doesn't understand your feedback, he or she won't be able to correct the error. Ask him or her to repeat the feedback and to explain and demonstrate how it will be used. If the athlete can't do this, be patient and present your feedback again. Then have the athlete repeat the feedback after you're finished.

Step 4: Provide an Environment That Motivates the Athlete to Improve. Your players won't always be able to correct their errors immediately even if they do understand your feedback. Encourage them to "hang tough" and stick with it when corrections are difficult or they seem discouraged. For more difficult corrections, remind them that it will take time, and the improvement will happen only if they work at it. Look to encourage players with low self-confidence. Saying something like, "You were hitting much better today; with practice, you'll be able to keep your head in and make consistent contact," can motivate a player to continue to refine his or her hitting skills.

Some athletes need to be more motivated to improve. Others may be very self-motivated and need little help from you in this area at all; with them you can practically ignore Step 4 when correcting an error. While motivation comes from within, look to provide an environment of positive instruction and encouragement to help your athletes improve.

A final note on correcting errors: Team sports such as softball provide unique challenges in this endeavor. How do you provide individual feedback in a group setting using a positive approach? Instead of yelling across the field to correct an error (and embarrassing the player), substitute for the player who erred. Then make the correction on the sidelines. This type of feedback has three advantages:

⊙ The player will be more receptive to the one-on-one feedback.

⊙ The other players are still active, still practicing skills, and unable to hear your discussion.

⊙ Because the rest of the team is still playing, you'll feel compelled to make your comments simple and concise—which, as we've said, is more helpful to the player.

This doesn't mean you can't use the team setting to give specific, positive feedback. You can do so to emphasize correct group and individual performances. Use this team feedback approach *only* for positive statements, though. Keep any negative feedback for individual discussions.

Developing Practice Plans

You will need to create practice plans for each season. Each practice plan should contain the following sections:

⊙ Purpose
⊙ Equipment
⊙ Plan

Purpose sections focus on what you want to teach your players during each practice; they outline your main theme for each practice. The purpose should be drawn from your season plan (see chapter 9). Equipment sections note what you'll need to have on hand for that practice. Plan sections outline what you will do during each practice session. Each consists of these elements:

⊙ Warm-up
⊙ Games
⊙ Skill practices
⊙ Cool-down and wrap-up

You'll begin each session with about five minutes of warm-up activities. Then you'll have your players play a modified softball game (look in chapter 8 for suggested games). You'll look for your cue to interrupt that game—your cue being when players are having problems with carrying out the basic goal or aim of the game. At this point you'll "freeze" the action, keeping the players where they are, and ask brief questions about the tactical problems the players encountered and what skills they need to solve those problems. (Review chapter 4 for more on interrupting a game and holding a question-and-answer session.)

Then you'll teach the skill the players need to acquire to successfully execute the tactic. During skill practice you'll use the IDEA approach:

- Introduce the skill.
- Demonstrate the skill.
- Explain the skill.
- Attend to players practicing the skill.

Your introduction, demonstration, and explanation of a skill should take no more than two to three minutes; then you'll attend to players and provide teaching cues or further demonstration as necessary as they practice the skill.

After the skill practices, you will usually have the athletes play another game or two to let them use the skills they have just learned and to understand them in the context of a game. During game and skill practices, emphasize the importance of every player on the field moving and being involved in every play, whether they will be directly touching the ball or backing up their teammates. No player on the field should be standing around.

The plan section continues with a cool-down and stretch. Following this you'll wrap up the practice with a few summary comments and remind them of the next practice or game day.

Most of the games in chapter 8 include lists of suggestions to help you modify each game to make it easier or harder to play. These suggestions will help you keep practices fun and provide activities for players with varying skill levels.

Although practicing using the games approach should reduce the need for discipline, there will be times when you'll have to deal with players who are misbehaving in practice. In the next section we'll help you handle these situations.

Dealing With Misbehavior

Athletes will misbehave at times; it's only natural. Following are two ways you can respond to misbehavior: through extinction or discipline.

Extinction

Ignoring a misbehavior—neither rewarding nor disciplining it—is called *extinction*. This can be effective under certain circumstances. In some situations, disciplining young people's misbehavior only encourages them to act up further because of the recognition they get. Ignoring misbehavior teaches youngsters that it is not worth your attention.

Sometimes, though, you cannot wait for a behavior to fizzle out. When players cause danger to themselves or others or disrupt the activities of others, you need to take immediate action. Tell the offending player that the behavior must stop and that discipline will follow if it doesn't. If the athlete doesn't stop misbehaving after the warning, discipline.

Extinction also doesn't work well when a misbehavior is self-rewarding. For example, you may be able to keep from grimacing if a youngster kicks you in the shin, but he or she still knows you were hurt. Therein lies the reward. In these circumstances, it is also necessary to discipline the player for the undesirable behavior.

Extinction works best in situations in which players are seeking recognition through mischievous behaviors, clowning, or grandstanding. Usually, if you are patient, their failure to get your attention will cause the behavior to disappear.

Be alert, however, that you don't extinguish desirable behavior. When youngsters do something well, they expect to be positively reinforced. Not rewarding them will likely cause them to discontinue the desired behavior.

Discipline

Some educators say we should never discipline young people, but should only reinforce their positive behaviors. They argue that discipline does not work, it creates hostility, and it sometimes develops avoidance behaviors that may be more unwholesome than the original problem behavior. It is true that discipline does not always work and that it can create problems when used ineffectively, but when used appropriately, discipline is effective in eliminating undesirable behaviors without creating other undesirable consequences. You must use discipline effectively, because it is impossible to guide athletes through positive reinforcement and extinction alone. Discipline is part of the positive approach when these guidelines are followed:

- Discipline in a corrective way to help athletes improve now and in the future. Don't discipline to retaliate and make yourself feel better.

- Impose discipline in an impersonal way when athletes break team rules or otherwise misbehave. Shouting at or scolding athletes indicates that your attitude is one of revenge.

- Once a good rule has been agreed upon, ensure that athletes who violate it experience the unpleasant consequences of their misbehavior. Don't wave discipline threateningly over their heads. Just do it, but warn an athlete once before disciplining.

- Be consistent in administering discipline.
- Don't discipline using consequences that may cause you guilt. If you can't think of an appropriate consequence right away, tell the player you will talk with him or her after you think about it. You might consider involving the player in designing a consequence.
- Once the discipline is completed, don't make athletes feel they are "in the doghouse." Make them feel that they're valued members of the team again.
- Make sure that what you think is discipline isn't perceived by the athlete as a positive reinforcement—for instance, keeping a player out of doing a certain drill or portion of the practice may be just what the athlete desired.
- Never discipline athletes for making errors when they are playing.
- Never use physical activity—running laps or doing push-ups—as discipline. To do so only causes athletes to resent physical activity, something we want them to learn to enjoy throughout their lives.
- Discipline sparingly. Constant discipline and criticism cause athletes to turn their interests elsewhere and to resent you as well.

Game-Day Coaching

Contests provide the opportunity for your players to show what they've learned in practice. Just as your players' focus shifts on contest days from learning and practicing to *competing*, so your focus shifts from teaching skills to coaching players as they perform those skills in contests. Of course, the contest is a teaching opportunity as well, but the focus is on performing what has been previously learned.

In the last chapter you learned how to teach your players softball tactics and skills; in this chapter we'll help you coach your players as they execute those tactics and skills in contests. We'll provide important coaching principles that will guide you throughout the game day—before, during, and after the contest.

Before the Contest

Just as you need a practice plan for what you're going to do each practice, you need a game plan for what to do on the day of a game. Many inexperienced coaches focus only on how they will coach during the contest itself, but your preparations to coach should include details that begin well before the first pitch of the game. In fact, your preparations should begin during the practice before the contest.

Preparations at Practice

During the practice a day or two before the next contest, you should do two things (besides practicing tactics and skills) to prepare your players: Decide on any specific team tactics that you want to employ, and discuss pregame particulars such as what to eat before the game, what to wear, and when to be at the field.

Deciding Team Tactics

Some coaches see themselves as great military strategists guiding their young warriors to victory on the battlefield. These coaches burn the midnight oil as they devise a complex plan of attack. There are several things wrong with this approach, but we'll point out two errors in terms of deciding team tactics:

1. The decision on team tactics should be made with input from players.
2. Team tactics at this level don't need to be complex.

Perhaps you guessed right on the second point but were surprised by the first. Why should you include your players in deciding tactics? Isn't that the coach's role?

It's the coach's role to help youngsters grow through the sport experience. Giving your athletes a chance to offer input here helps them to learn the game. It gets them involved at a planning level that often is reserved solely for the coach. It gives them a feeling of ownership; they're not just "carrying out orders" of the coach. They're executing the plan of attack that was jointly decided. Youngsters who have a say in how they approach a task often respond with more enthusiasm and motivation.

Don't dampen that enthusiasm and motivation by concocting tactics that are too complex. Keep tactics simple, especially at the younger levels. On the offensive side, focus on moving runners along and employing smart baserunning. On the defensive side, focus on making sure of getting one out, getting the lead runner whenever possible, making good cutoffs and relays, and throwing to the proper base.

As you become more familiar with your team's tendencies and abilities, help them focus on specific tactics that will help them play better. For example, if your team has a tendency to stand around and watch the action, emphasize moving into position to back up hits and throws. If they execute backups well but often miss the cutoff player (perhaps in trying to make too long a throw) and throw to the wrong base, emphasize proper positioning on cutoffs, teamwork, and communication.

If you're coaching 12- to 14-year-olds, you might institute certain plays that your team has practiced. These plays should take advantage of your players' strengths. Again, give the players the chance to provide input into what plays might be employed in a game.

Discussing Precontest Particulars

Players need to know what to do before a contest: what they should eat on game day and when, what clothing they should wear to the game, what equipment they should bring, and what time they should arrive at the field. Discuss these particulars with them at the practice before a contest. Here are guidelines for discussing these issues.

Pregame Meal. Carbohydrates are easily digested and absorbed and are a ready source of fuel. Players should eat a high-carbohydrate meal ideally about three to four hours before a game to allow the stomach to empty completely. This won't be possible for games held in early morning; in this case, athletes should still eat food high in carbohydrates, such as an English muffin, toast, or cereal, but not so much that their stomachs are full. In addition, athletes' pregame meals shouldn't include foods that are spicy or high in fat content.

Clothing and Equipment. Instruct players to wear their team shirts or uniforms and suitable shoes with rubber cleats.

Time to Arrive. Your players will need to adequately warm up before a game, so instruct them to arrive 20 minutes before a game to go through a team warm-up (see "The Warm-Up" later in this chapter).

Facilities, Equipment, and Support Personnel

Although the site coordinator and umpires have responsibilities regarding facilities and equipment, it's wise for you to know what to look for to make sure the contest is safe for the athletes. You should arrive at the field 25 to 30 minutes before game time so you can check the field, check in with the site coordinator and umpires, and greet your players as they arrive to warm up. The site coordinator and umpires should be checking the facilities and preparing for the contest. If umpires aren't arriving before the game when they're supposed to, inform the site coordinator. A facilities checklist includes the following:

Field surface

✔ Sprinkler heads and openings are at grass level.

✔ The field is free of toxic substances (lime, fertilizer, and so on).

✔ The field is free of low spots or ruts.

✔ The playing surface is free of debris.

✔ No rocks or cement slabs are on the field.

✔ The field is free of protruding pipes, wires, and lines.

✔ The field is not too wet.

✔ The field is not too dry.

✔ The field lines are well marked.

Outside playing area

✔ The edge of the playing field is at least six feet from trees, walls, fences, and cars.

✔ Nearby buildings are protected (by fences, walls) from possible damage during play.

✔ Storage sheds and facilities are locked.

✔ The playground area (ground surface and equipment) is in safe condition.

✔ The fences/walls lining the area are in good repair.

✔ Sidewalks are without cracks, separations, or raised concrete.

Spectators

✔ Areas for spectators are clearly marked.

✔ Spectators have adequate protection from flying objects.

Equipment

✔ The backstop is secured to the ground.

✔ The backstop is well behind the playing area.

✔ Fences are marked with a warning track.

Unplanned Events

Part of being prepared to coach is to expect the unexpected. What do you do if players are late? What if *you* have an emergency and can't

Communicating With Parents

The groundwork for your communication with parents will have been laid in the parent orientation meeting, through which parents learn the best ways to support their kids'—and the whole team's—efforts on the field. As parents gather at the field before a contest, let them know what the team has been focusing on during the past week and what your goals are for the game. For instance, perhaps you've worked on the cutoffs and relay throws in practice this week; encourage parents to watch for improvement and success in executing these plays and to support the team members as they attempt all tactics and skills. Help parents to judge success not just based on the contest outcome, but on how the kids are improving their performances.

If parents yell at the kids for mistakes made during the game, make disparaging remarks about the umpires or opponents, or shout instructions on what tactics to employ, ask them to refrain from making such remarks and to instead be supportive of the team in their comments and actions.

After a contest, briefly and informally assess with parents, as the opportunity arises, how the team did based not on the outcome, but on meeting performance goals and playing to the best of their abilities. Help parents see the contest as a process, not solely as a test that's pass/fail or win/lose. Encourage parents to reinforce that concept at home.

make the game or will be late? What if the game is rained out or otherwise postponed? Being prepared to handle out-of-the-ordinary circumstances will help you when such unplanned events happen.

If players are late, you may have to adjust your starting lineup. While this may not be a major inconvenience, do stress to your players the importance of being on time for two reasons:

- Part of being a member of a team means being committed and responsible to the other members. When players don't show up, or show up late, they break that commitment.

- Players need to go through a warm-up to physically prepare for the contest. Skipping the warm-up risks injury.

Consider making a team rule stating that players need to show up 20 minutes before a game and go through the complete team warm-up, or they won't start.

An emergency might cause *you* to be late or miss a game. In such cases, notify your assistant coach, if you have one, or the league coordinator. If notified in advance, a parent of a player or another volunteer might be able to step in for the contest.

Sometimes a game will be postponed because of inclement weather or for other reasons (such as unsafe field conditions). If the postponement takes place before game day, you'll need to call each member of your team to let him or her know. If it happens while the teams are on the field preparing for the game, gather your team members and tell them the news and why the game is being postponed. Make sure all your players have rides home before you leave—be the last to leave to be sure.

The Warm-Up

Players need to both physically and mentally prepare for a game once they arrive at the field. Physical preparation involves warming up. We've suggested that players arrive 20 minutes before the game to warm up. Conduct the warm-up similar to practice warm-ups, with some brief games that focus on skill practice and stretching.

Players should prepare to do what they will do in the game: run, catch, throw, pitch, and hit. This doesn't mean they spend extensive time on each skill; you can plan two or three brief practice games that encompass all these skills. Have your starting pitcher warm up on the sidelines with the starting catcher.

After playing a few brief games, your players should stretch. You don't need to deliver any big pep talk, but you can help your players mentally prepare as they stretch by reminding them of the following:

- The tactics and skills they've been working on in recent practices, especially focusing their attention on what they've been doing well. Focus on their strengths.
- The team tactics you decided on in your previous practice.
- Performing the tactics and skills to the best of their individual abilities and playing together as a team.
- Playing hard and smart and having fun!

During the Contest

The list you just read goes a long way toward defining your focus for coaching during the contest. Throughout the game, you'll keep the game in proper perspective and help your players do the same. You'll observe how your players execute tactics and skills and how well they play together. You'll make tactical decisions in a number of areas. You'll model appropriate behavior on the bench, showing respect for opponents and umpires, and demand the same of your athletes. You'll watch out for your athletes' physical safety and psychological welfare in terms of building their self-esteem and helping them manage stress and anxiety.

Proper Perspective

Winning games is the short-term goal of your softball program; helping your players learn the tactics, skills, and rules of softball, how to become fit, and how to be good sports in softball and in life is the long-term goal. Your young athletes are "winning" when they are becoming better human beings through their participation in softball. Keep that perspective in mind when you coach. *You* have the privilege of setting the tone for how your team approaches the game. Keep winning and all aspects of the competition in proper perspective, and your young charges will likely follow suit.

Tactical Decisions

While you aren't called upon to be a great military strategist, you are called upon to make tactical decisions in several areas throughout a contest. You'll make decisions about who starts the game and when to enter substitutes; about making slight adjustments to your team's tactics; and about correcting players' performance errors or leaving the correction for the next practice.

Starting and Substituting Players

In considering playing time, make sure that everyone on the team gets to play at least half of each game. This should be your guiding principle as you consider starting and substitution patterns. Check your league rules for substituting players; you might be able to remove a starter once from a game and have that player re-enter once.

Adjusting Team Tactics

At the 8 to 9 and 10 to 11 age levels, you probably won't adjust your team tactics too significantly during a game; rather, you'll focus on the basic tactics in general and emphasize between innings which tactics your team needs to work on in particular. However, coaches of 12- to 14-year-olds might have cause to make tactical adjustments to improve their team's chances of performing well and winning. As games progress, assess your opponents' style of play and tactics and make adjustments that are appropriate—that is, that your players are prepared for. Consider the following examples:

- Does the pitcher use a high leg kick or not pay attention to baserunners? If so, you might want to have runners steal more often.

- Does the opposing team's offense revolve around a couple of key hitters? If this is the case, you might instruct your pitcher to "pitch around" those hitters—not give them anything good to hit.

- Is the opposing team's defense shoddy, especially in the area of cutoffs and relays? This might prompt you to gamble on the bases more, trying to take the extra base.

- Is the opposing pitcher overpowering? You might instruct your batters to cut down on their swings, try to go to the opposite field, and even lay down a bunt or two.

Don't stress tactics too much during a game, however. Doing so can take the fun out of the game for the players. If you don't trust your memory, carry a pen and notepad to note which team tactics and individual skills need attention in the next practice.

Correcting Players' Errors

In chapter 5 you learned about two types of errors: learning errors and performance errors. Learning errors are ones that occur because athletes don't know how to perform a skill. Athletes make performance errors not because they don't know how to do the skill, but because they make a mistake in executing what they do know.

Sometimes it's not easy to tell which type of error athletes are making. Knowing your athletes' capabilities helps you to know whether they know the skill and are simply making mistakes in executing it or whether they don't really know how to perform the skill. If they are making learning errors—that is, they don't know how to perform the skills—you'll need to make note of this and teach them at the next practice. Game time is not the time to teach skills.

If they are making performance errors, however, you can help players correct those errors during a game. Players who make performance errors often do so because they have a lapse in concentration or motivation—or they are simply demonstrating the human quality of sometimes doing things incorrectly. A word of encouragement to concentrate more may help. If you do correct a performance error during a contest, do so in a quiet, controlled, and positive tone of voice between innings or when the player is on the bench with you.

For those making performance errors, you have to decide if it is just the occasional error anyone makes or an expected error for a youngster at that stage of development. If that is the case, then the player may appreciate your not commenting on the mistake. The player knows it was a mistake and knows how to correct it. On the other hand, perhaps an encouraging word and a "coaching cue" (such as "Remember to rotate the shoulder and hip—don't bail out!") may be just what the athlete needs. Knowing the players and what to say is very much a part of the "art" of coaching.

Coach's and Players' Behavior

Another aspect of coaching on game day is managing behavior—both yours and your athletes'. The two are closely connected.

Your Conduct

You very much influence your players' behavior before, during, and after a contest. If you're up, your players are more likely to be up. If you're anxious, they'll notice and the anxiety can be contagious. If you're negative, they'll respond with worry. If you're positive, they'll play with more enjoyment. If you're constantly yelling instructions or commenting on mistakes and errors, it will be difficult for players to concentrate. Instead, let players get into the flow of the game.

The focus should be on positive competition and on having fun. A coach who overorganizes everything and dominates a game from the bench is definitely *not* making the contest fun.

So how should you conduct yourself on the bench? Here are a few pointers:

- Be calm, in control, and supportive of your players.
- Encourage players often, but instruct during play sparingly. Players should be focusing on their performance during a game, not on instructions shouted from the bench.
- If you need to instruct a player, do so in an unobtrusive manner when you're both on the bench. Never yell at players for making a mistake. Instead, briefly demonstrate or remind them of the correct technique and encourage them.

Remember, you're not playing for a World Series ring! In this program, softball competitions are designed to help players develop their skills and themselves—and to have fun. So coach at games in a manner that helps your players do those things.

Players' Conduct

You're responsible for keeping your players under control. Do so by setting a good example and by disciplining when necessary. Set team rules of good behavior. If players attempt to cheat, fight, argue, badger, yell disparaging remarks, and the like, it is your responsibility to correct the misbehavior. Consider team rules in these areas of game conduct:

- Players' language
- Players' behavior
- Interactions with umpires
- Discipline for misbehavior
- Dress code for competitions

Players' Physical Safety

We devoted all of chapter 3 to discussing how to provide for players' safety, but it's worth noting here that safety during contests can be affected by how umpires are calling the rules. If they aren't calling rules correctly, and this risks injury to your players, you must intervene. Voice your concern in a respectful manner and in a way that places the emphasis where it should be: on the athletes' safety. One of the umpires' main responsibilities is to provide for athletes' safety; you are not adversaries here. Don't hesitate to address an issue of safety with an umpire when the need arises.

Players' Psychological Welfare

Athletes often attach their self-worth to winning and losing. This idea is fueled by coaches, parents, peers, and society, who place great emphasis on winning. Players become anxious when they're uncertain if they can meet the expectations of others or of themselves when meeting these expectations is important to them.

If you place too much importance on the game or cause your athletes to doubt their abilities, they will become anxious about the outcome and their performance. If your players look uptight and anxious during a contest, find ways to reduce both the uncertainties about how their performance will be evaluated and the importance they are attaching to the game. Help athletes focus on realistic personal goals—goals that are reachable and measurable and that will help them improve their performance, such as staying focused on defense and providing good cutoffs on throws from the outfield. Another way to reduce anxiety on game day is to stay away from emotional pregame pep talks. We provided guidance earlier in what to address before the game.

When coaching during contests, remember that the most important outcome from playing softball is to build or enhance players' self-worth.

Keep that firmly in mind, and strive to make every coaching decision promote your athletes' self-worth.

Opponents and Umpires

Respect opponents and umpires. Without them, you wouldn't have a competition. Umpires help provide a fair and safe experience for athletes and, as appropriate, help them learn the game. Opponents provide opportunities for your team to test itself, improve, and excel.

You and your team should show respect for opponents by giving your best efforts. You owe them this. Showing respect doesn't necessarily mean being "nice" to your opponents, though it does mean being civil.

Don't allow your players to "trash talk" or taunt an opponent. Such behavior is disrespectful to the spirit of the competition and to the opponent. Immediately remove a player from a contest if he or she disobeys your orders in this area.

Remember that umpires are quite often teenagers—in many cases not much older than the players themselves. The level of officiating should be commensurate to the level of play. In other words, don't expect perfection from umpires any more than you do from your own players.

After the Contest

When the game is over, join your team in congratulating the coaches and players of the opposing team, then be sure to thank the umpires. Check on any injuries players sustained and let players know how to care for them. Be prepared to speak with the umpires about any problems that occurred during the game. Then hold a brief Team Circle, as explained in a moment, to ensure your players are on an even keel, whether they won or lost.

Winning With Class, Losing With Dignity

When celebrating a victory, make sure your team does so in a way that doesn't show disrespect for the opponents. It's fine and appropriate to be happy and celebrate a win, but don't allow your players to taunt the opponents or boast about their victory. Keep winning in perspective. Winning and losing are a part of life, not just a part of sport. If players can handle both equally well, they'll be successful in whatever they do.

Athletes are competitors, and competitors will be disappointed in defeat. If your team has made a winning effort, let them know that.

After a loss, help them keep their chins up and maintain a positive attitude that will carry over into the next practice and contest.

Team Circle

If your players have performed well in a game, compliment them and congratulate them immediately afterward. Tell them specifically what they did well, whether they won or lost. This will reinforce their desire to repeat their good performances.

Don't criticize individual players for poor performances in front of teammates. Help the players improve their skills, but do so in the next practice, not immediately after a game.

The postgame Team Circle isn't the time to go over tactical problems and adjustments. The players are either so happy after a win or so dejected after a loss that they won't absorb much tactical information immediately following a game. Your first concern should be your players' attitudes and mental well-being. You don't want them to be too high after a win or too low after a loss. This is the time you can be most influential in keeping the outcome in perspective and keeping them on an even keel.

Finally, make sure your players have transportation home. Be the last one to leave in order to help if transportation falls through and to ensure full supervision of players before they leave.

chapter 7

Rules and Equipment

This is where we'll introduce you to some of the basic rules of softball. We won't try to cover all the rules of the game, but rather will give you what you need to work with players who are 8 to 14 years old. We'll give you information on terminology, equipment, field size and markings, player positions, and game procedures. We recommend you use these rules, many of which have been modified from the adult version of the game to make the sport more appropriate for youngsters. In a short section at the end of the chapter we'll show you the officiating signals for softball.

Terms to Know

Softball has its own vocabulary. Being familiar with common terms will make your job easier. In some cases we go into more depth on terms to explain related rules.

balance point—The point in the pitching delivery at which the throwing hand is at its highest point above the head, the glove-side foot is at its highest point above the ground, and the weight is in the center of the body.

balk—An illegal motion by the pitcher resulting in runners advancing one base.

ball—A pitch that the batter doesn't swing at and that is outside of the strike zone.

baserunner—An offensive player who is either on base or attempting to reach a base.

batter's box—Rectangles on either side of home plate designating the area in which a batter must stand.

batting rules—A batter cannot leave the batter's box once the pitcher becomes set or begins the windup. Both feet must be inside the batter's box (the lines are part of the box). If the batter hits the ball—either fair or foul—with one or both feet on the ground entirely outside of the box, the batter is automatically out. Also, a batter may request time, but the umpire does not have to grant the request. If a batter refuses to take position in the batter's box, the umpire will order the pitcher to pitch and call each pitch a strike, no matter the location.

bunt—A method of hitting accomplished by holding the bat so that the pitch is hit softly, traveling several feet in front of home plate or down the first- or third-base line. Batters attempting to bunt on the third strike are out if the ball is picked up in foul territory. This play is considered a strikeout.

choking up—Moving the hands up the bat handle to increase bat control.

count—The number of balls and strikes on a hitter.

crow hop—Use of the body and arm in a throwing motion that generates maximum velocity on the ball.

defensive interference—The baseline belongs to the runner. A fielder not in the act of fielding cannot block the path of the runner between any bases. In such a case the ball is dead and the runner is awarded the base he or she would have reached, in the umpire's judgment, had he or she not been obstructed.

double—A hit that allows the batter to reach second base safely.

double play—A defensive play that results in putting two players out.

dropped third strike—If first base is unoccupied, or if it is occupied with two out, and the catcher drops a third strike, the defensive team must put out the batter by either throwing to first before the batter reaches the base or by tagging the batter with the ball before he or she reaches first.

error—A defensive mistake that enables a runner to advance or reach a base safely that the player would otherwise have been unable to advance to or would have been put out before reaching.

fair territory—The area of the playing field between (and including) the foul lines.

fielder's choice—A situation that allows a batter to reach a base safely because a fielder decides to put out a different baserunner.

fly ball—A hit that sails high into the air; also known as a *pop fly.*

fly-out—A fly ball that is caught, resulting in the batter being put out.

force play—Occurs when a runner is forced to advance to the next base because the batter becomes a runner and the preceding base is occupied. On a ground ball, runners are forced to run in these situations: first base occupied; first and second occupied; first, second, and third occupied; first and third occupied (only the runner on first is forced to run). On force plays, the defender needs to touch the base while in possession of the ball before the runner reaches the base to record an out. An out resulting from a force play is called a *force-out.*

foul ball—Any ball hit into foul territory. Note, though, that a ground ball that is fair as it passes first or third base and then rolls into foul territory is a fair ball.

foul line—Either of the two straight lines extending at right angles from the rear of home plate through the outer edges of first and third bases to the outfield boundary. A batted ball that lands on a foul line is considered to have landed in fair territory.

foul territory—The area of the playing field that lies beyond the foul lines.

foul tip—A ball that is tipped by the batter and either caught or dropped by the catcher. With two strikes on the batter, a foul tip must be caught by the catcher for an out (a strikeout) to be recorded; otherwise the batter may still bat.

ground ball—A hit that bounces or rolls along the ground; also known as a *grounder.*

ground-out—A ground ball that is fielded by an infielder, resulting in the batter being put out at first base.

hit by a pitch—A batter is awarded first base for being hit by a pitch.

home run—A home run is recorded when a batter hits a fair ball over the fence or circles the bases on an inside-the-park hit without being thrown out.

infield—The part of the playing field enclosed by the three bases and home plate.

infield fly rule—This rule prohibits a player from intentionally dropping a fair fly ball that can be caught in the infield with normal effort. This rule is in effect with runners on first and second, or first, second, and third, with less than two outs. When an umpire calls an infield fly rule, the batter is automatically out and runners may advance at their risk.

inning—A division of a game that consists of each team having a turn at bat.

offensive interference—A runner is out if he or she intentionally interferes with a thrown ball, hinders a fielder from making a play on a batted ball, or intentionally interferes with a fielder or the ball in trying to break up a double play. In this case both the runner and the batter are out.

out—An out can be recorded in a variety of ways, including strikeout, force-out, tag-out, and fly-out.

outfield—The part of the playing field outside the infield and between the foul lines.

overthrow—When a base is overthrown and the ball goes out of play (such as over a fence or in a dugout), runners are awarded the next base.

passed ball—A pitch not hit by the batter that passes the catcher and should have been caught (see *wild pitch*). Typically passed balls pass the catcher in the air before bouncing. To be a passed ball, a baserunner must advance on the play.

pitching rules—Once a pitcher begins his or her motion to home with any runners on base, he or she must throw or be called for a balk. With the bases empty, a pitcher has 20 seconds to pitch or the umpire will automatically call a ball. A ball is also called when the pitcher brings his or her pitching hand into contact with his or her mouth or lips while on the mound (exceptions may be made in cold weather); for applying a foreign substance to the ball; for spitting on the ball, either hand, or the glove; and for rubbing the ball on the glove, body, or clothing. The pitcher may rub the ball in his or her bare hands. Pitchers cannot intentionally throw at a batter. A manager or coach may make two trips to the mound during an inning to talk to the pitcher; on the second trip, the pitcher must be removed.

put-out—A batter/runner or baserunner is called out (such as with a force-out or tag-out).

run—The basic unit of scoring that is credited each time a baserunner advances safely to home plate.

running out of the baseline—A runner is out when she or he runs out of the baseline, which is more than three feet away from a direct line between the bases, unless she or he is doing so to avoid interfering with a fielder fielding a batted ball.

running past first base—Runners are entitled to run past first base without risking being tagged out. They give up this right if they turn toward second base, however. Once they turn toward second, they can be tagged out.

sacrifice bunt—A bunt that results in the batter being put out, though the baserunner(s) advance(s).

sacrifice fly—A fly-out that results in a run being scored.

scoring position—Second or third base, from which a baserunner could score on a base hit.

single—A hit that allows the batter to reach first base safely.

squeeze play—With a runner on third base the batter bunts to allow the runner to safely score.

strike—A pitch that the batter takes (doesn't swing at) in the strike zone; that the batter swings at and misses; or that the batter hits into foul territory.

strikeout—A batter being put out as the result of having a third strike.

strike zone—The area over home plate through which a pitch must pass to be called a strike, between the top of the knees and the midpoint between the top of the shoulders and the top of the pants (see figure 7.1).

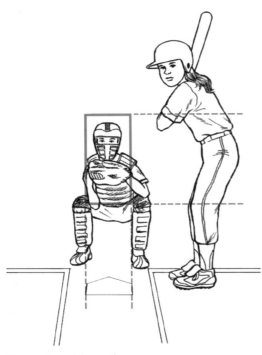

Figure 7.1 The strike zone.

tag play—Occurs when a runner is not forced to advance (see *force play*). When a runner is not forced to advance, such as with a runner on second, the runner must be tagged out (touched with the ball, which can be in a fielder's glove or bare hand) when the runner is not touching a base.

tag up—The action of a baserunner who contacts his or her base after a fly ball has been caught, with the intention of advancing to the next base. A runner cannot advance to the next base on a caught fly ball until the fly ball is caught.

triple—A hit that allows the batter to reach third base safely.

triple play—A defensive play that results in putting three players out.

walk—A batter advancing to first base as the result of having a fourth ball. Also called a base on balls.

wild pitch—A pitch not hit by the batter that passes the catcher and could not have been caught (see *passed ball*). Typically wild pitches are those that are in the dirt before they pass the catcher. To be considered a wild pitch, a baserunner must advance on the play.

Rule Modifications

Table 7.1 shows modified rules for softball. Note that in fast-pitch (FP), each team has 9 players participating; in slow-pitch (SP), teams have 10 players participating, adding a short fielder to the outfield.

Field

Softball is played on a diamond-shaped field, with home plate and first, second, and third bases forming the corners. Foul lines run from home to first base and home to third base and extend beyond those bases to the outfield fence. The area inside the foul lines, including the lines, is fair territory; anything outside the lines is foul. Fair territory around the base portion of the field is called the infield. Fair territory in the grassy portion of the field farther from the plate is called the outfield (see figure 7.2).

Equipment

You're probably aware of most standard pieces of equipment: bases, balls, bats, gloves, helmets, and other appropriate apparel. But do you know how to tell when this equipment meets proper specifications and is in good repair? Here are some tips.

Table 7.1 Rule Modifications for Softball

Item	8- to 9-year-olds	10- to 11-year-olds	12- to 14-year-olds
Players on field per team	9 (FP) 10 (SP)	9 (FP) 10 (SP)	9 (FP) 10 (SP))
Players on team	15	15	15
Basepaths	55 ft	60 ft	60 ft
Pitching distance	35 ft	35 ft	40 ft
Fence	150 ft	175 ft	175 ft
Ball	11-inch ball	11-inch ball	11-inch ball
Pitcher	Coach	Player	Player
Pitching restrictions	None	6 innings per game; 10 per week	7 innings per game; 10 per week
Innings	6	6	7
10-run rule	Yes (after 4 innings)	Yes (after 4 innings)	Yes (after 5 innings)
Leadoffs	No	No	No
Steals	No	Yes (FP) No (SP)	Yes (FP) No (SP)
Designated hitter	No	No	No

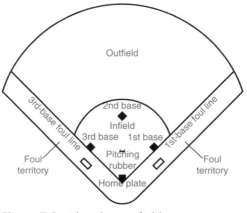

Figure 7.2 The playing field.

Bases

Be sure that your organization uses breakaway bases. Because as many as 70 percent of softball injuries occur when players slide, you owe it to youngsters to make the bases as safe as possible.

Balls

Standard softballs are 11 inches in circumference. We suggest that these be used for all age groups.

Bats

The bat is divided into three parts: the knob, the handle, and the barrel (see figure 7.3). Bats must be all wood or all aluminum. Rubber sheaths are permitted on aluminum bat knobs and handles to improve the grip. Legal aluminum bats are made of one piece, and some have a plug in the barrel end. A bat with a large hitting end tapering down to a small handle gives the greatest sweet spot—that is, the greatest area with which to make solid hits. The handle of the bat should be thin enough that the player can easily grip both hands around it. After that, it's up to the players' personal preferences what bat they feel most comfortable using.

Figure 7.3   Parts of the bat.

Gloves

No piece of equipment will become more dear to your players than their gloves. Help your players select proper-fitting gloves. It's better to start with a smaller glove than an oversized one. A mitt that has a huge pocket and is much bigger than a youngster's hand will be hard to control and could hinder skill development.

   Breaking in, or conditioning, a glove will help create a good pocket and make the glove strong and flexible. Players can rub some hot water or saddle soap into the centers of their gloves, stuff a couple of softballs or a large wad of crumpled newspaper into the pockets, and then

Figure 7.4 Use shoelaces to help break in your glove.

use shoelaces to tie the gloves (see figure 7.4). Leaving the mitts like this for several days will create good, round pockets. Well-conditioned gloves will improve your players' ability to field and hold onto the ball.

Apparel

Your players must wear helmets while batting and running the bases. An on-deck player (the player who will be hitting next) must also wear a helmet, as should players serving as base coaches. We recommend helmets certified by the National Operating Committee on Standards for Athletic Equipment (NOCSAE), with double flaps. Check to make sure your players' helmets fit and that the condition of each helmet is good.

Players should also wear softball shoes with rubber cleats. Double-tying the laces of the shoes will prevent them from coming untied, which can cause a player to trip. Players should wear caps to keep hair and sun out of their eyes.

Some positions require special equipment. The catcher will need a face mask, helmet, throat guard, chest protector, and shin guards.

Don't allow players to wear jewelry, watches, or other metal objects during practice and games. This helps prevent injury.

Player Positions

Fast-pitch softball is played with 9 players in the field on defense; slow-pitch softball has 10.

The pitcher and catcher, known as the *battery*, are the busiest defensive players. *Infielders*, who handle ground balls and pop-ups on the dirt portion of the field, include the first-base player, second-base player, shortstop, and third-base player. The *outfielders* are the right fielder, center fielder, and left fielder. In slow-pitch softball, a short fielder is also stationed in the outfield (see figure 7.5).

One of your biggest coaching decisions involves answering the question: Who should play which position? Here are some tips to help you choose wisely:

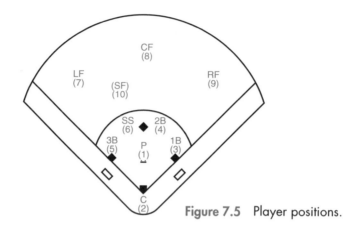

Figure 7.5 Player positions.

⊙ Set your lineup to maximize your players' strengths and interests.

⊙ Put your best defensive players "up the middle" at catcher, pitcher, middle infielders (second base and shortstop), and center fielder.

⊙ Give your players experience at a variety of positions throughout the season to expand their skills and understanding of the game. You might be surprised when a player exhibits skills at one position that were not evident at a previous defensive spot.

The following specific suggestions should help you determine where on the field each player should play. Included with each position is the number associated with it.

⊙ **Pitcher (1)**—Arm strength or velocity is an indication that a player may make a successful pitcher. A solid mental and emotional makeup will also make a pitcher effective, because a pitcher must stay poised throughout the game. Your pitcher should be a smart, tough, and confident competitor who will rise to the occasion when confronting a challenge. The player must be able to throw strikes; control is the number one priority. Spend a lot of time with your pitchers.

⊙ **Catcher (2)**—The catcher is the team's "quarterback." All the action takes place in front of this player. Good catchers are rugged individuals, and if they are not big and strong, then they must be tough. The position requires strength, endurance, and great hand-eye coordination. The catcher is up and down from a squat position on every pitch, throwing balls back to the pitcher or infielders, backing up first base on ground balls when other runners aren't on base, and chasing short foul balls. The catcher must field the position, throw the ball, and lead the team.

⊙ **First base (3)**—The ability to catch all types of thrown balls is essential for a first-base player. Size, powerful hitting, speed, grace of movement, good fielding of ground balls, and good judgment of infield flies are other qualities of a good first-base player. The first-base player makes more unusual plays than any other position. A strong and accurate arm is a bonus at this position.

⊙ **Second base (4)**—Players of all different statures have become excellent second sackers. Whether big or little, however, a second-base player must have a sure pair of hands to field ground balls, pop flies, and thrown balls. Moreover, a second-base player must be able to foresee fielding situations and act instantly.

⊙ **Third base (5)**—The third-base player must possess agility, good hands, and quick reflexes. This player must be able to come in fast on the ball and throw accurately while running at top speed. She or he must be able to make off-balance throws and bare-handed pickups on bunts and slowly hit balls. The third-base player must have a strong arm to make the long throws to first base.

⊙ **Shortstop (6)**—A shortstop must be alert, be able to start and stop quickly, possess a sure pair of hands, and, above all, have a strong throwing arm. This player must also have quick reactions. The shortstop will be required to make more tough plays than any other player on the field.

⊙ **Left field (7)**—The left fielder can have less speed and a weaker arm than any other outfielder because many of the throws do not cover a great distance. However, this player must still be alert, have a good arm to the plate, and be a good fielder of ground balls. The left fielder backs up third base whenever necessary.

⊙ **Center fielder (8)**—This player usually has the best speed of the outfielders and must have a strong arm. The center fielder covers more territory than any other player and will make the greatest percentage of outfield put-outs. The center fielder backs up at second base on all sacrifice bunts and every attempted put-out at second.

⊙ **Right field (9)**—The right fielder must have a strong, accurate throwing arm. This player backs up first base on all bunted balls, all throws from the catcher to first base, and all plays when there is a possibility of the ball's coming into right field, such as on a wild throw. The right fielder also backs up at second base on all balls hit to the left side of the diamond.

⊙ **Short field (SF)**—The short fielder is used in slow-pitch softball only. This player should be fast, sure-handed, and an accurate thrower to get to, catch, and relay balls hit past the infielders.

Softball Game Procedures

Knowledge of the basic rules and procedures of softball will ensure that the game runs smoothly. Be aware of any special rules for the playing field or boundaries. Here are some elements common to softball games:

- The home team (the team that bats second) usually is predetermined by league officials; if it has not been, flip a coin to determine the home team.
- A game is divided into innings. Each team gets one turn at bat per inning. See table 7.1 for our recommendations for the number of innings played at each age level.
- Pitchers must throw the ball underhand with a very small arc in fast-pitch and with a 6- to 12-foot arc in slow-pitch (see figure 7.6).
- The batting order must be followed throughout the game unless a player is substituted for another. Substitutes must take the same place in the batting order as the replaced player.
- Each batter is allowed a maximum of three strikes or four balls (upon the fourth ball, the batter is awarded first base). Many slow-pitch leagues start each batter with a 1-ball, 1-strike count.
- A batter who avoids making an out and safely reaches first base, in hitting the ball, has a hit (or has reached base on a fielder's error). The player may try to advance to another base.
- A batter makes an out by striking out (three strikes), grounding out (the ball touches the ground before being caught and is thrown to

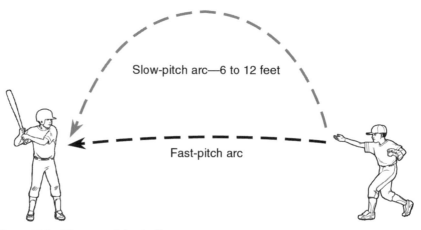

Figure 7.6 The arc of the ball.

first base before the batter arrives), or flying out (the ball is caught by a fielder before it touches the ground).

◎ A run is scored if an offensive player reaches first, second, and third bases and home plate without being tagged out or forced out (a defensive player with the ball touches the base before the runner arrives, and the runner cannot retreat to the previous base because a teammate is already advancing there). The offensive player can overrun (run past) first base without being able to be tagged out.

◎ A baserunner cannot leave a base until the pitcher releases the ball.

◎ With the third out, a team's turn at bat ends. That team takes the field, and the opposing team bats.

◎ The team with the most runs at the end of the game is the winner.

◎ Extra innings are played to determine the winner if a game is tied at the end of regulation play.

◎ In slow-pitch softball, a tenth position—short fielder—is added to both team's lineups.

Keeping Score

Using a scorebook is easy once you know the numbering system (see "Player Positions" on pages 74-76) and a few abbreviations.

AB—Times at bat

B—Bunt

BB—Base on balls; walk

BK—Balk

DP—Double play

E—Error

F—Foul fly

FC—Fielder's choice

FO—Fly-out

G—Ground ball (unassisted infield out)

H—Hit

HBP—Hit by pitch

IW—Intentional walk

K—Strikeout

Kc—Called third strike

L—Line drive

O—Out

OS—Out stealing

PB—Passed ball

R—Run

SH—Sacrifice

SB—Stolen base

TP—Triple play

WP—Wild pitch

Every time a batter goes to the plate, use the numbers to indicate how the player was retired or reached base. For instance, the batter who grounds to the shortstop and is thrown out at first base is scored 6-3 in your scorebook (see figure 7.7a). If he or she flies to the right fielder, use FO-9 (see figure 7.7b). If the batter fouls out to the right fielder, use 9F. If a batter reaches first base on an error made by the second-base player, steals second, goes to third on a wild pitch, and scores on a passed ball, your scorebook would look like figure 7.7c.

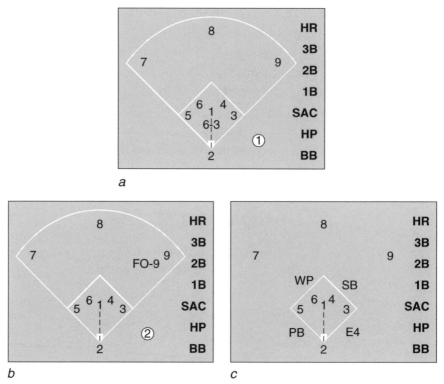

Figure 7.7 Scorebook samples for fast-pitch softball.

Umpires

Umpires are officials who enforce the rules of the game. At this level, games usually have two umpires—one at home plate and another positioned according to the number of baserunners and bases they occupy. Before the game, the home plate umpire meets with both coaches to exchange their lineups. Umpires decide whether a pitch is a ball or strike, a hit is fair or foul, and if a runner is safe or out. The home plate umpire is the ultimate decision-maker on any ruling.

Like you, umpires are volunteers, not professionals. Consequently, from time to time they will make mistakes. How you react when you think an umpire has erred is important. Be a good role model for your players. If you think a rule was not properly enforced, calmly call time-out and discuss it with the umpire. Don't mutter about the call in the dugout or interrupt the game by arguing. Remember, you are not allowed to contest judgment calls (ball-strike, safe-out, fair-foul), only rules interpretations. See figure 7.8a-f for common umpires' signals.

Figure 7.8 Some signals commonly used by umpires are *(a)* time-out, *(b)* strike, *(c)* out, *(d)* safe, *(e)* foul, and *(f)* fair.

chapter 8

Tactics and Skills

As your athletes play games in practice, their experiences in these games—and your subsequent discussions with them about their experiences—will lead them to the tactics and skills they need to develop to succeed. In the games approach, teaching tactics and teaching skills go hand in hand.

In this chapter we'll provide information to help you teach your players team tactics and individual offensive and defensive skills. We'll also include suggestions for identifying and correcting common errors. Remember to use the IDEA approach to teaching skills—introduce, demonstrate, explain the skill, and attend to players practicing the skill. For a refresher on IDEA, see chapter 5.

If you aren't familiar with softball skills, rent or purchase a video to see the skills performed. While this chapter ties directly to the season plans in chapter 9, describing the tactics and skills that you'll teach in practices, it also includes skills not earmarked to be formally taught. Use these additional skill descriptions as reference points. You may also find advanced books on skills helpful.

We've only provided information about the basics of softball in this book. As your players advance in their skills, you'll need to advance your knowledge as a coach. You can do so by learning from your experiences, watching and talking with more experienced coaches, and studying advanced resources.

Offensive Tactics

The offensive tactics you teach should never exceed your players' abilities to perform the necessary skills. However, given that your players understand and can perform the required individual skills, you can teach them a variety of basic strategies and develop their sense of when to use those strategies. Here is a list of the offensive tactics you might teach your team. (Note that leagues at certain levels may not allow all these tactics; check your league rules book.)

○ **Steal**—When a baserunner takes off for the next base on the pitch and advances safely to the base. Considerations include watching the delivery of the pitcher, getting a jump on the pitch, running hard, and sliding to avoid the tag.

○ **Delayed steal**—Similar to a straight steal, except the runner waits until the catcher's attention is diverted or relaxed. For instance, a runner may wait to take off until a catcher begins to lazily lob the ball back to the pitcher. By the time the pitcher can catch the throw, the runner can be safely sliding into the base. Another opportunity to use the delayed steal is when the middle infielders do not cover second base after the pitch.

○ **Double steal**—Like a straight steal, except two runners are involved. One version of the double steal calls for the trailing runner to break for the next base and draw a throw. The lead runner then breaks quickly for the next base.

○ **Hit-and-run**—When a runner takes off on the pitch and the batter makes contact with the ball. This helps break up double play possibilities and move runners into scoring position. Don't use this strategy if the opposing pitcher is wild (thus making it difficult for the batter to make contact) or if the hitter is not skilled enough to make frequent contact.

○ **Drag bunt**—Requires slightly different footwork from the bunting technique described on pages 120-121, but the basic difference between the two is that a drag bunter waits longer to drop down from a hitting to a bunting position. This strategy is best used if the first or third base player is playing deep.

○ **Sacrifice bunt**—Like a regular bunt, except the batter's sole responsibility is to lay down a bunt so a baserunner can advance successfully. The batter will most likely be thrown out at first, but the lead runner will be one base closer to home.

○ **Sacrifice fly**—When a batter hits a fly ball that scores a runner from third. Young hitters will have difficulty doing this intentionally, and you should discourage hitters from doing it if you think it may cause them to drop the back shoulder habitually. More often than not, a sacrifice fly just happens in the course of trying for a hit, rather than being planned strategy.

○ **Hit to opposite field**—Generally used in two instances: when a coach wants the hitter to advance a runner and when a hitter is always trying to "pull" the ball or is swinging too hard. (A right-handed batter pulls the ball by hitting it down the third base line or to left field.) By concentrating on hitting to the opposite field, the hitter will see the ball longer and won't swing as hard.

○ **Take on 3-0 count**—A good strategy against a pitcher who is struggling to get the ball across the plate. The hitter takes the pitch in hopes of getting a free pass to first base.

Offensive Tactics Games

FAST FEET

Goal

To steal a base

Description

Play 4v4, with a pitcher, catcher, second-base player, and shortstop (see figure 8.1). The offense has a runner on first and a batter at the plate, but the batter does not swing. When the pitcher pitches, the runner on first takes off for second (adhere to your league rules in

(continued)

Fast Feet *(continued)*

terms of taking leadoffs and leaving the bag; don't allow an excessive leadoff even though there is no first-base player). The catcher attempts to throw the runner out. Rotate runners until each runner gets three steal attempts, then rotate teams. Keep track of points—one point for every stolen base.

To make the game easier

◎ Allow the runner a leadoff if none was granted earlier.

◎ Allow the runner to take off on the pitch if that was not allowed earlier.

To make the game harder

◎ Don't allow leadoffs if they were allowed earlier.

◎ Don't allow the runner to take off on the pitch if that was allowed earlier. Instead, the runner must wait until the ball gets to the plate.

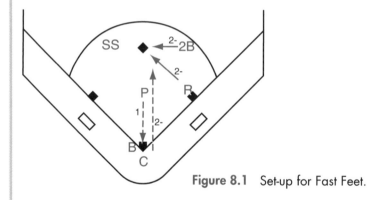

Figure 8.1 Set-up for Fast Feet.

HIT AND RUN

Goal

To execute the hit-and-run play

Description

Play 3v10 or 3v9. Set up an entire defense and place one runner on first base (see figure 8.2). Pitch easy pitches to hit, and have the batter attempt to hit to right field to move the runner up. The runner should advance as far as possible without being thrown out. Let each set of three offensive players have two at-bats each, then rotate in three players from the defense. Award points this way:

- Two points for a hit that advances a runner to third or home.
- One point for a hit that advances a runner only to second.
- Zero points for plays that do not advance the runner.

To make the game easier
- Have batters hit off a tee.
- Instruct infielders to let the ball go through to the outfield.
- Allow leadoffs.

To make the game harder
- Pitch harder pitches.
- Allow no leadoffs.

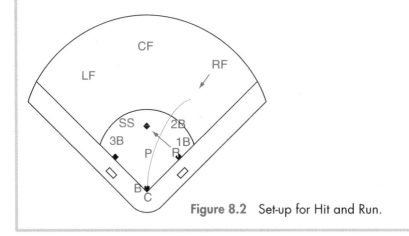

Figure 8.2   Set-up for Hit and Run.

Signals to Players

Develop a simple system of hand signals to set plays in motion, and teach your players that a sign stays on until you signal that it no longer applies. Have your players watch the entire series of signs instead of picking up a sign and turning immediately to the batter's box, because you may still be giving additional decoy signs.

Don't overload your players, however. If they have trouble grasping a tactic or remembering a signal, simplify or drop it. Consider making the "real" sign the first sign you give. Players can't execute what they can't understand. Table 8.1 shows a sample of some hitting and base-running signals you might use (see also figure 8.3).

In addition, instruct your players to react to situations that allow them to take advantage of the defense, even when you haven't called a specific

Table 8.1 Coaches' Signs

	Sign	Message
To batters	Right hand across chest	Swing away
	Right hand to nose	Take pitch
	Right hand to belt	Bunt
	Right hand to ear	Sacrifice bunt
	Rubbing hands together	Wipe-off sign
To baserunners	Left hand to face	Steal
	Left hand to bill of cap	Delayed steal
	Left hand pointing	Double steal
	Left hand patting top of cap	Stay, unless a wild pitch, passed ball, or hit
	Left hand across chest	Go on contact

Figure 8.3 Hitting and baserunning signals.

play. For example, if a catcher loses control of a pitch, your baserunners should be ready to take the next base without your telling them to do so.

You may also need to shout instructions to baserunners when a defensive player loses the flight of the ball. Think ahead each time a batter comes up to bat, keeping in mind

- the speed of your baserunners,
- the strength of the infielders' and outfielders' arms,
- playing conditions, and
- the score.

Hitting Strategies

The batter, more than any other offensive player, dictates the offensive strategy. You will more likely tell baserunners to run with the pitch if you have a good contact hitter at the plate who has limited power than with a power hitter up who strikes out a lot. Why?

The contact hitter will probably get the bat on the ball, preventing a "strike-'em-out, throw-'em-out" double play (a strikeout and a caught stealing). Second, the batted ball often won't make it out of the infield, making it easier to get a force-out if the lead runner is not moving on the pitch. But with a power hitter up, you don't want to take the chance that she or he will swing and miss and leave the baserunner an easy target for the catcher. And because the power hitter is likely to get the ball beyond the infield if contact is made, there is not a big advantage to sending the runner, because a force-out is unlikely.

A good hitter should observe the pitcher during warm-ups and on pitches to teammates who bat earlier in the lineup. The hitter can also ask teammates for information about the speed, location, and type of pitches thrown.

Once in the batter's box, the hitter must always be aware of the count, the number of outs, and the coach's signal. A missed sign can result in an easy double play. In contrast, a sign that is received and executed can be the start of a big inning. So go over all these signals regularly during your practices. Make corrections when a sign is missed so it doesn't happen in a game.

A good hitter is a confident hitter. You can boost any player's hitting confidence by staying positive. If you're praying for a hitter to walk because you doubt he or she can get the bat on the ball, then what do you suppose the team is thinking? Be positive, even when your lineup is retired one, two, three.

Baserunning Strategies

For your players to be effective baserunners, they must know how, when, and why to remain at a base or try to advance. Here are a few simple rules about baserunning:

⊙ **Watch the pitcher.** Instruct your players to watch the hurler prepare to pitch the ball. Once the pitcher strides toward home plate, she or he cannot throw to a base, so your baserunner can increase the leadoff or try to steal. However, if the pitcher steps toward first base or moves his or her back foot off the rubber, your runner should quickly return to the bag.

⊙ **Listen to and watch the base coach.** Explain that the base coach's job is to watch what's going on in the field and help players run the bases safely. Runners on first base should listen to instructions from the first-base coach; runners on second and third base should follow the instructions of the third-base coach.

⊙ **Do not run unless you are forced to.** Baserunners are not always forced to run. For example, if a runner is on first base and a fly ball is caught in the outfield, the runner is not forced to go to second base. She or he can stay at first base. The base coach will tell the baserunners when a force is in effect.

⊙ **Stay close to the base and tag up on fly balls.** At the 8- to 9-year-old level, you can send runners halfway to the next base on fly balls to the outfield because about as many fly balls will be dropped as caught. However, if a fly ball is caught, a runner who has left a base must tag up (touch the base he or she was occupying before the play started) before advancing.

Baserunning Game

FIRST TO THIRD

Goal

To show good judgment in running the bases. A secondary goal—for the defense—is to execute proper relays.

Description

Put three or four defensive players in the outfield and three more in the infield (at second base, third base, and shortstop). Line up the other players at first base; they will rotate in as runners (see figure 8.4).

Hit singles to the outfield, and the runners attempt to go from first to third base. Award one point each time a runner reaches third base safely. If runners judge they cannot make it to third, they should stay at second. Switch groups after each runner has gone twice.

To make the game easier for runners

⊙ Hit balls between the outfielders.

To make the game easier for fielders

⊙ Hit balls straight at the outfielders.

To make the game harder for runners

⊙ Bring the outfielders closer in.

To make the game harder for fielders

⊙ Have three offensive players at first base and three at home plate as runners. One runner attempts to go from first to third; the other goes from home plate to second base. Award the offense one point when a player reaches third base and one point if the player who starts at home base reaches second base. Take away a point for an out recorded at either base.

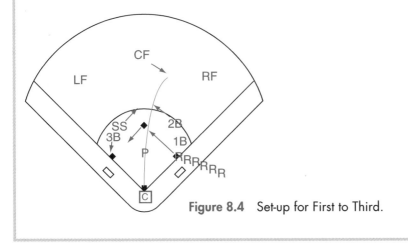

Figure 8.4 Set-up for First to Third.

Defensive Tactics

Effective team defense starts with teaching players how to correctly position themselves, provide backups, execute relays and cutoffs, and make specific defensive plays.

Positioning

Positioning is a primary concern of any team defense. In softball, it's not as simple as telling your players, "If your opponent does this, you do that." Instead, you'll have to base your positioning instructions on the hitter's preferred batting side and his or her tendencies.

For example, say the batter at the plate is a left-hander and a pull hitter (typically hitting the ball to the right side of second base). Given this, you'd want your fielders to shade toward the right side of the diamond (see figure 8.5).

Shifting to the right or left is not all there is to consider about defensive positioning. You'll also want players to move up or back, depending on the hitter's estimated power. Additional elements of good team defense through positioning include backing each other up on the field and efficiently relaying and cutting off throws from the outfield.

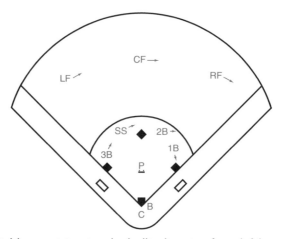

Figure 8.5   Fielders anticipating the ball's direction for a left-handed pull hitter.

Backups

In most games and practices, a few throws inevitably get by the fielders. That's why every fielder has backup responsibilities.

It isn't so much the initial mistake that hurts, but rather the series of mistakes that follow if a backup isn't used. In other words, a bad throw to third isn't critical unless no one is there to back up the play, and the ball rolls all the way to the fence (see figure 8.6). What should have been either an out at third or a runner safe at third turns into a run.

Figure 8.6   Backups can prevent mistakes and save runs.

Error Detection and Correction for Backups

ERROR   Players stand around when the ball is not hit to them.

CORRECTION   Make sure all players know where to move on any given play. Walk them through their repositioning for a variety of plays. Set up game situations that require players to react quickly. Make it a fun game by calling out situations and seeing who can get to their proper positions the fastest.

Relays and Cutoffs

Relays and cutoffs are very important in team defense. Typically, the shortstop and second-base player are responsible for moving out to receive throws from the outfielders and relaying them to the appropriate base. The shortstop handles all relay throws from the left and center fielders, while the second base player takes throws from the right fielder (see figure 8.7a-b).

When a fly is hit deep to an outfielder, the appropriate infielder runs toward the outfielder and lines up with the base to which the infielder intends to relay the throw (see figure 8.8). The weaker the outfielder's arm, the closer the infielder needs to get to the outfielder.

A cutoff player gets in a position between the fielder throwing the ball and the base where the play is to be made. For example, if a runner will definitely reach the next base before a throw reaches the base, the ball should be cut off before it reaches the base (see figure 8.9). The player cutting off the throw either relays the throw to the base or throws to another base to make a play on a trailing runner.

Cutoff players should position themselves 15 to 25 feet ahead of the base where the play is to be made. Most throws that are cut off are to third base or home plate. The third base player is the cutoff player on throws from left field to home, and the first base player takes all throws from center field and right field to home (see figure 8.10a-b). The short-stop is the cutoff player for throws to third base (see figure 8.11), and the pitcher backs up these throws either at third or home.

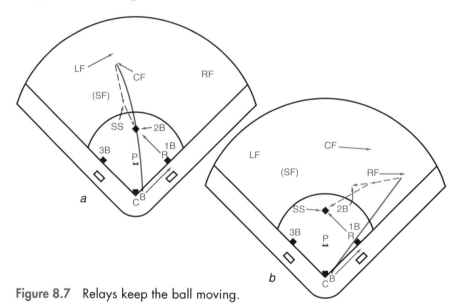

Figure 8.7 Relays keep the ball moving.

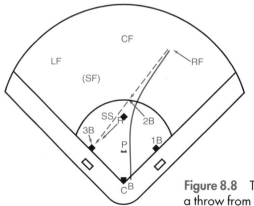

Figure 8.8 The second-base player relays a throw from the right fielder to third base.

Figure 8.9 Use a cutoff when a runner will be safe before the ball reaches the base.

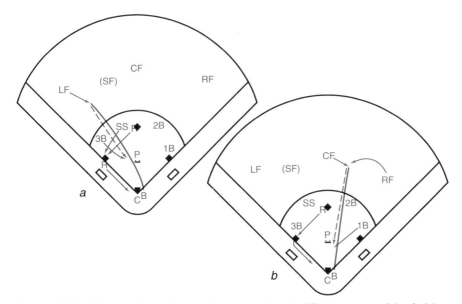

Figure 8.10 First- and third-base players work with different parts of the field to cut off the play.

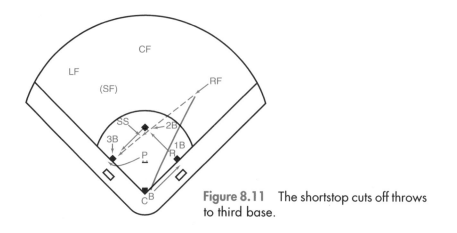

Figure 8.11 The shortstop cuts off throws to third base.

Relay Game

HIT THE RELAY

Goal

To execute efficient relay throws

Description

This game is for three players. Assign the players to right field, second base, and third base (see figure 8.12). Have the coach hit or throw the ball so the right fielder needs to move to get it, then complete the relay to third base.

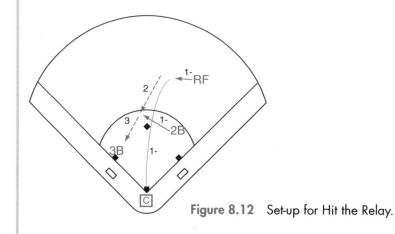

Figure 8.12 Set-up for Hit the Relay.

Award one point for a throw caught in the air by the second-base player. Award one point for the relay to third base in which the third-base player catches the ball either straddling the bag or with one foot touching the side of the bag. After the players have scored six points, rotate them to different positions.

To make the game easier

⊙ Have the coach make shorter hits.

To make the game harder

⊙ Add a runner on first base who is attempting to go to third.

Force Plays

A force play occurs when a baserunner must go to the next base on a ground ball because the batter has become a baserunner (e.g., a batter running to first on a ground ball forces a runner to go to second, because you can't have two runners on one base). Runners are not forced to advance to the next base on balls caught in the air. Runners who are forced to advance, however, are put out when the defense gets the ball to the base ahead of the runner. A defensive player must be in possession of the ball and touching the base (typically with a foot, but not necessarily so) before the runner arrives for the runner to be put out (see figure 8.13).

Figure 8.13 A force out at second.

A force play can be made at all three bases and home plate. The basic techniques are the same, regardless of the base. The player throwing the ball should make the throw about chest-high. The player covering the base should move to the side of the base nearest the source of the throw (see figure 8.14). This shortens the throw's length and, thus, the time it takes to arrive, making it more likely an out will be made.

Once the throw is on the way and the covering player knows where the throw will arrive, that player should place one foot on the base and stretch out to meet the throw with the glove hand and the other foot (see figure 8.15). If the throw is slightly off target to the side, the player should step to meet the ball with the foot on the ball side and contact the base with the other foot. If the play is going to be close, the player should stretch as far as she or he can and catch the ball in the glove hand only. If the play is not going to be close, the player should stretch a comfortable distance and catch the ball with both hands. The player catching the ball should always look to shorten the distance and time of the throw so the throw will get there before the runner does.

Figure 8.14 The covering player moving toward a throw.

Figure 8.15   Stretch out to meet a throw.

Force Play Game

LEAD RUNNER

Goal

To execute force plays at second base

Description

Play 6v6. Field an entire infield. The offense begins with a runner on first (see figure 8.16). Pitch balls that are easy to hit. Batters hit grounders; the defense tries to make force plays at second. Each batter hits until he or she hits a ground ball. Each play begins with a runner on first. All six batters for the offense take one turn hitting, then they go through their rotation and hit one more ground ball each (so they hit 12 ground balls in all). Then switch the offense and defense and repeat the game. Score one point for the defense for every force made at second; score two points if they turn a double play.

(continued)

Lead Runner *(continued)*

To make the game easier

○ Don't allow leadoffs.

○ Don't allow the runner to take off on the pitch. Instead, the runner must wait until the ball gets to the plate.

○ Have batters hit off a tee.

○ Hit or throw the ball yourself to locations that will make the play easier.

To make the game harder

○ Allow leadoffs.

○ Allow the runner to take off on the pitch.

○ Hit or throw the ball yourself to locations that will make the play difficult.

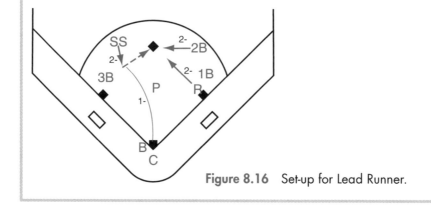

Figure 8.16   Set-up for Lead Runner.

Tag Plays

The tag play is another fundamental defensive concept. A tag play situation occurs any time a runner is not in contact with a base and is not allowed to move to any base freely. For example, a runner overrunning second base can return safely to second by retouching the base before being tagged. To put out a baserunner with a tag play, the defensive player must tag or touch the runner with the ball, or with the glove holding the ball, when the runner is off the base (see figure 8.17).

The tag play is required when a runner is not forced to advance to the next base. Examples of tag play situations include a runner

Figure 8.17   The defense tags out a runner.

- ⊙ on second base (with no runner on first base) who runs on a ground ball,
- ⊙ on second base who attempts to score on a base hit, or
- ⊙ tagging up on a fly ball who attempts to advance to the next base.

Note that in the first example, if there had been a runner on first as well as second, it would have been a force play, because the runners would have been forced to advance on a ground ball.

The throw for a tag play should arrive just below the knees of the covering player (see figure 8.18). The runner will probably be sliding into the base, so the throw should be low and close to the runner. This minimizes the time it takes for the covering player to move the glove and ball into position to tag the runner.

More than one technique is acceptable for covering a base on a tag play. The recommended method places the covering player in position at the base where he or she can tag the runner with limited chances of being knocked down. As players' skills increase, they can actually block the base from the runner with their bodies as they make the tag. But begin by teaching a method that limits the chances of collision.

Figure 8.18   Fielder in good position for tag play.

The covering player's position at the base depends on the paths of the runner and the incoming ball. In general, the player should straddle the base or stand just to the side of the base facing the direction of the incoming runner (see figure 8.19a-b). Players should never place a leg between the base and the incoming runner. They should leave the path to the base open to the runner.

Covering players should position themselves so that they can catch the ball and bring the gloved ball down to the edge of the base where the runner will arrive. As the runner slides in, the player should let the runner tag himself or herself out by sliding into the gloved ball. The player should then sweep the ball out of the way of the runner to avoid losing control of the ball. If the runner doesn't slide, the runner's foot will be the first part of the runner to touch the base, so the covering player should tag the foot (see figure 8.20). When the player reaches out to tag the chest of an incoming runner who doesn't slide, the runner is often safe because he or she has gotten a foot on the base first.

When a defensive player tags out a runner who is running past him or her between bases, the defensive player should hold the ball securely with both hands with the ball in the glove and tag the runner with the back of the fingers of the glove (see figure 8.21). The fielder should then pull both hands away immediately so the contact doesn't knock the ball out of the glove.

a   b

Figure 8.19 Covering the base for a tag play by *(a)* straddling the base or *(b)* standing to the side of the base facing the direction of the incoming runner.

Figure 8.20 A runner tagged on the foot.

Figure 8.21   A runner tagged out between bases.

Tag Play Game

TAG-OUT

Goal

To tag out baserunners

Description

This game involves six players; get two games going at once to keep all players involved. Place defenders at second base, third base, short-stop, and right field. Place a runner on second base (see figure 8.22). Another runner will alternate with that runner, each one running every other play. Each play starts with the runner on second. The runner must attempt to go to third on each play. Alternate hits—hit fly-outs to the right fielder in which the runner must tag up, and hit ground balls to second base and shortstop. (Don't hit to third, as the runner wouldn't attempt to advance in such a situation.) The defense tries to get the runner out at third base; if the runner is tagged out, the defense scores a point. After six plays, rotate the two baserunners with two defenders.

To make the game easier

⊙ Don't use an outfielder.

⊙ Don't allow leadoffs.

To make the game harder

⊙ Allow leadoffs.

⊙ Hit the ball to spots that will make the play difficult.

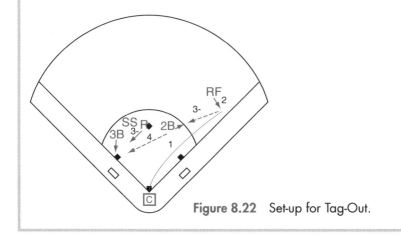

Figure 8.22   Set-up for Tag-Out.

Double Plays

Double plays occur any time two runners are put out during continuous action. Examples include a fly-out, in which the baserunner is put out after failing to tag up or is tagged out at the next base after correctly tagging up; a strikeout and a runner thrown out on the same play trying to steal; and a ground ball with a runner on first, with force-outs made at second and first bases. Double plays are rally-killers for the offense and morale boosters for the defense. They are also more difficult to execute, because there are usually more players handling the ball, more throws made, and thus more time used. However, as your players advance in their skills, they can learn to execute double plays.

With less than two outs and a runner or runners in force situations, the first option is usually to cut down the lead runner. Once the lead runner is put out at one base, the covering player at that base throws to first base to complete the double play. Here we'll focus on executing the second-to-first double play.

Shortstop Drag

On ground balls hit to the right side of second base and most ground balls hit to the pitcher, the shortstop will cover second base; that is, the shortstop will take the throw from the fielder fielding the ball, drag his or her foot across the base, and make the relay throw to first base to complete the double play. The keys to covering the base when throws are made by the first- or second-base player from the outfield side of the baseline between first and second base are these:

1. Move just behind second base, straddling the back corner of the bag (the corner pointing to center field) with the inside of the right foot (see figure 8.23a).

2. Face the thrower.

3. If there is no time to straddle the bag, move through that position without stopping.

4. As you catch the ball and make the force-out, step toward the right outfield grass with your left foot, dragging the toes of your right foot across the back corner of the base (see figure 8.23b).

5. Throw to first base (see figure 8.23c).

a   b

Figure 8.23   Shortstop drag.

c

Figure 8.23 *(continued)*

Shortstop Inside Pivot

On balls fielded by the pitcher or catcher, the shortstop covers second and uses an inside pivot to make the force-out and complete the throw to first. Here are the keys for making an inside pivot:

1. Step on the inside corner of the base with the left foot, facing the player with the ball (see figure 8.24a).
2. Bend the knees as you catch the ball, place weight fully on the left foot, and spring off that foot toward the pitcher's mound, landing on the right foot out of the path of the runner (see figure 8.24b).
3. Step toward first and make the throw (see figure 8.24c).

Second-Base Pivots

On ground balls hit to the left side of second base, the second-base player must use either a crossover pivot or a rocker pivot. He or she uses a crossover pivot on any throw from the third-base player and long throws from the shortstop. A rocker pivot is used on short throws by the short-stop.

Figure 8.24 Shortstop inside pivot.

Here are the keys to making the crossover pivot:

1. Cover second so you can cross the base in a direct line toward the player feeding you the ball (see figure 8.25a).
2. If time allows, move to a position just short of the base, facing the thrower.
3. As the ball approaches, step on the base with your left foot, move over the base, and catch the ball on the far side of the base while still in contact with it (see figure 8.25b).
4. Stop your forward momentum by landing on your right foot; with this step you should be out of the basepath.
5. Shift your weight to the left side; step left and throw to first (see figure 8.25c).

a

b

c

Figure 8.25   Second-base player's crossover pivot.

Here are the keys to executing the rocker pivot:

1. Move to the base and place the toes of your right foot in contact with the outfield side of the base (see figure 8.26a).
2. With the weight on your left foot, catch the ball, make the force-out, step back onto the right foot (see figure 8.26b), step left toward first base, and throw the ball (see figure 8.26c).

a

b

c

Figure 8.26   Second-base player's rocker pivot.

Players can also execute the rocker pivot by standing with their weight on their *right* foot, kicking the base with their *left* foot for the force-out, and stepping left to throw. This move is quicker by one step, but leaves the fielder in the baseline. If the runner is far away, this version of the rocker pivot is fine to use.

Double Play Game

DOUBLE TROUBLE

Description

Play 6v6. Field an entire infield. The offense begins with a runner on first (see figure 8.27). Pitch balls that are easy to hit. Batters hit grounders; the defense tries to make a double play. Each batter hits until he or she hits a ground ball. Each play begins with a runner on first. All six batters for the offense hit one ground ball, then they go through their rotation and hit one more ground ball (so they hit 12 ground balls in all). Then switch the offense and defense and repeat the game. Score one point for the defense for every force made at second; score two points if they are able to turn a double play.

To make the game easier

- Don't allow leadoffs.
- Don't allow the runner to take off on the pitch. Instead, the runner must wait until the ball gets to the plate.
- Have batters hit off a tee.
- Hit or throw the ball yourself to locations that will make the play easier.

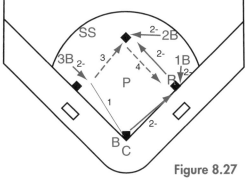

Figure 8.27 Set-up for Double Trouble.

(continued)

Double Trouble *(continued)*

To make the game harder

- ◎ Allow leadoffs.
- ◎ Allow the runner to take off on the pitch.
- ◎ Hit or throw the ball yourself to locations that will make the play difficult.

Rundowns

Rundown situations occur when a runner is caught between bases by the defense. When one runner is in a rundown and another runner is on third base, the defense needs to keep an eye on the runner on third, who may try to score. Fielders must be ready to throw the ball home to cut down the runner trying to score.

The two defenders closest to the bases between which the runner is caught are the primary defenders; the two fielders next closest to these bases are backup fielders in the rundown. Backup fielders should stay at least 10 feet behind the primary fielders unless the play has moved close to a base. If a primary fielder throws the ball to a teammate, the player who threw the ball becomes a backup fielder as the player backing him or her up assumes a primary fielding role. Here are keys to executing a rundown:

1. The fielder with the ball initiates the play by holding the ball up, ready to throw, and running directly at the baserunner until the runner commits to moving toward one base or the other.

2. If this first fielder can't make the tag, the ball is thrown to the player toward whom the runner is going.

3. The runner should be forced to run back to the last base, rather than forward to the next base. For example, a runner caught between third base and home should be forced to run back toward third.

4. Try to get the runner out with one throw. Two throws are all right, but more than two are too many, opening the gate for errors or for other runners advancing. Throws should be by the side of the runner, rather than over the runner's head (see figure 8.28).

5. Tag the runner with the ball in the glove, not just held in the hand. In fact, it's preferable to use the bare hand to cover the ball in the glove to make sure it's secure.

Figure 8.28   The proper throw for a rundown.

Rundown Game

PICKLE

Goal

To execute effective rundowns

Description

Set up four stations placed about 30 feet apart. Each station consists of two bases placed 30 feet apart (see figure 8.29). Designate one base to be second base and one to be third. Assign three players to each station, two fielders and one runner. The runner starts in a rundown and then tries to reach a base safely.

Award points to the defense using the following system:

- Two points for getting the runner out going back to second base
- One point for getting the runner out going forward to third base
- Zero points if the runner reaches second base safely
- Minus one point if the runner reaches third base safely

(continued)

Pickle *(continued)*

When a rundown is completed, restart by having the runner begin halfway between the bases again. Players rotate whenever the defensive players at that station score four points.

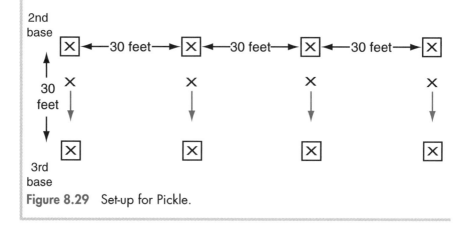

Figure 8.29 Set-up for Pickle.

Other Defensive Plays

In addition to the plays we've already talked about, your players need to know other plays to execute well defensively. Consider introducing the following defensive tactics to your team:

◉ **Get the lead runner.** The lead runner is the one farthest advanced on the bases. The defense's objective is to stop the player closest to scoring by throwing the ball to the base ahead of the lead runner (see figure 8.30).

◉ **Look the runner back.** On ground balls in certain tag play situations, a fielder can look a runner back to the base before throwing to first for the out, thus keeping the runner from advancing. For example, when a runner is on second and a ground ball is hit to the third-base player, that fielder should field the ball (focusing entirely on fielding it first!), and as he or she begins the throwing motion, look quickly at the runner to "freeze" the runner from advancing. Unless the runner tries to advance, the fielder should not stop or slow the throwing motion. If the runner does try to advance, the fielder is ready to make a play on the runner. If the fielder doesn't pay attention to the runner, the runner likely will be able to advance.

◉ **Back up the throw.** Every player not directly involved in a play should back up throws to different parts of the field. The pitcher backs

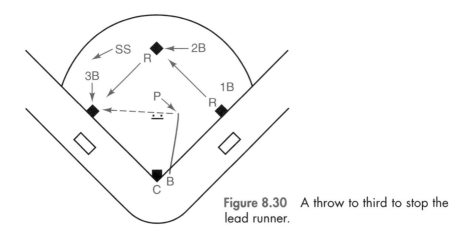

Figure 8.30 A throw to third to stop the lead runner.

up the base that the lead runner is moving toward, especially if it's home plate. Infielders back up each other when a throw is coming from the catcher.

⊙ **Back up the hit.** Outfielders not directly involved in a play back up each other. If the ball gets away from one outfielder, the backup can make the play and prevent runners from taking an extra base.

⊙ **Give up a run.** Sometimes you'll decide to give up a run in exchange for an out because you have a comfortable lead. In this case you might let a runner on third score on a ground ball to get the easier out at first.

⊙ **Get the first out.** In a double play situation, the first out must be the lead runner. If infielders retire the lead runner, they can attempt to complete the double play.

Again, keep your defensive strategies simple and the number manageable. Defense requires quick reactions. If you overload players with too much information or it's too difficult, they won't be able to respond quickly and properly when the ball is hit.

Pitching Strategies

You've probably heard the distinction between a pitcher and a thrower. A pitcher is a surgeon, exposing each hitter's weakness. (Every hitter has at least one.) The pitcher rarely throws the ball far from the strike zone and thus seldom walks a batter.

In contrast, a thrower simply rears back and fires the ball at the catcher's mitt, figuring the velocity of the pitch will prevent the hitter from making contact. Throwers walk many hitters because of their wildness.

Teach your pitchers to pitch, not just throw. Help them to understand why they shouldn't lob the ball right over the plate when the count is 3-1. Along with a pitching mind-set, help pitchers develop their mechanics early; they'll have more success and fewer arm problems.

Offensive Skills

Offensive skills include hitting and baserunning. Hitting a ball is probably the most difficult skill to master in fast-pitch softball. Combine this fact with your players' ages and inexperience, and you've got your work cut out for you. Helping your players improve their hitting fundamentals will certainly make their experience more rewarding. And baserunning is just as vital to a successful offense. Unfortunately, many youth teams get runners on base, then make inning-ending baserunning blunders. These next two sections should help you coach your players to be better hitters and baserunners.

Hitting

Good hitters perform the skill in one fluid motion. However, four separate hitting components should be taught to young players: grip, stance, stride, and swing.

Grip

Teach your players to grip the bat with their fingers, not with the palms of their hands (middle knuckles should be lined up; see figure 8.31). They should hold the bat loosely until they get ready to swing; then they should tighten the grip.

Stance

Players need to be comfortable in the batter's box. The stance that feels good to one player may feel awkward to another. Figure 8.32 shows an appropriate stance. Don't try to make every batter assume the same stance at the plate, but do stress these basics:

- Feet comfortably wider than shoulders, set in a square stance
- The back foot parallel to the back line of the batter's box

Figure 8.31   The proper way to grip the bat.

Figure 8.32   Proper stance at the plate.

- The front foot parallel with the front line of the box, toes pointing toward the plate
- Knees bent slightly with weight centered on the balls of the feet, distributed 60 percent over the back foot and 40 percent over the front
- Upper body bent slightly at the waist, eyes focused on the ball
- Bat held at a 45-degree angle to the hands
- Elbows out from the body and flexed, pointing down toward the ground
- Feet far enough back from the plate so the bat passes slightly across the outer edge of the plate when the arms are fully extended

Stride

The hitter starts by rotating the front shoulder, hip, and knee inward. This is the trigger motion. The slight rotation causes the hands to move three to four inches backward. The hip rotation and the turning of the knee inward cause the player's weight to shift to 60 percent over the front foot and 40 percent over the back foot. A hitter doesn't need to stride to hit. As the saying goes, "Bury the toe and put on a show."

However, if a player does stride, it should be very small. The weight is on the inside part of the back foot after a player completes the stride, and the hands are cocked in a trigger position just off the back shoulder. If a player is going to stride, be sure he or she strides *before* contact, not at contact.

Swing

The legs and hips initiate the swing. As the hitter shifts the weight to the front foot, the back foot pivots and the back knee rotates. During this sequence there is a transfer of weight from the back foot onto the front foot, resulting in 60 percent being over the front foot and 40 percent being over the back foot. The front foot remains straight and firm, the shoulders open, and the hands come down and through (see figure 8.33). The hitter should keep the barrel of the bat level with or above the hands during the swing. The lead elbow points toward the ground. The hitter should keep the head still during the swing. The bat should be parallel to the ground as it moves through the hitting zone. Teach your players to hit down and through the ball.

Figure 8.33   The proper swing stance.

Error Detection and Correction for Hitting

ERROR   A hitter overstrides and lunges at the ball.

CORRECTION   Have the player widen his or her stance and reduce or eliminate the stride.

ERROR   A hitter doesn't pivot on the back foot.

CORRECTION   Tell the hitter to raise the heel of the back foot off the ground and turn the foot in a little.

ERROR   A hitter pulls his or her head and front shoulder away from the pitch.

CORRECTION   Have the pitcher throw to a catcher while the hitter in the box follows the path of the ball to the catcher's mitt.

ERROR   A hitter swings late.

CORRECTION   Instruct the hitter to begin the trigger motion sooner.

ERROR   A hitter takes good cuts but always misses the ball.

CORRECTION   Remind the player to keep his or her head still to keep an eye on the ball and to bury his or her chin in the back shoulder as he or she finishes the swing.

Slow-Pitch Hitting Adjustments

The same basic fast-pitch hitting mechanics apply to slow-pitch soft-ball. However, because the ball is pitched slower and with a much higher arc, slow-pitch hitters should take advantage of their additional reaction time.

Hitting to a certain spot (e.g., behind a runner) is easier in slow-pitch, because hitters can make adjustments in their stance. For example, a hitter who is in a squared stance (see figure 8.34a) when the pitcher releases the ball can move the front foot forward to close the stance (see figure 8.34b). By doing so, the hitter can more easily hit the ball to the opposite field, if he or she is patient enough to wait on the pitch.

Also unlike the fast-pitch hitters, a hitter in slow-pitch may swing level or even drop the back shoulder and uppercut on the ball (see figure 8.35). Again, this depends on the game situation and the ideal location for the ball to be hit in the field of play.

a   b

Figure 8.34 The proper slow-pitch stances (a) squared stance, (b) closed stance.

Figure 8.35 Dropping the back shoulder to upper-cut the ball.

Hitting Game

HITTING DOWN

Goal

To encourage players to hit down on the ball and emphasize contact

Description

Play 4v4 with defensive players at first, second, and third bases and at shortstop (see figure 8.36). Each play begins with a runner on first base; all four players on offense will bat once. Place a batting tee at home plate. The batter must hit a ground ball. The defense attempts to force the runner at second base.

Award the offense one point if the runner is safe at second base and another point if the runner is safe at first base. Switch the offense and defense after each player on the offensive team has batted.

To make the game easier

⊙ Have no runners on base. The offense gets a point if the batter/runner is safe at first.

(continued)

Hitting Down *(continued)*

To make the game harder

⊙ Use live pitching.

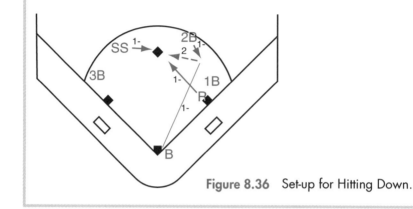

Figure 8.36 Set-up for Hitting Down.

Bunting

Every team needs a variety of offensive weapons. One of these weapons is the bunt. So teach every player on your team how to bunt, and provide practice time so each player feels confident about the skill. The main purpose of the bunt is to advance baserunners, but it's also a good surprise strategy to get on base. The bunt is a good tactic for your players to use against overpowering pitchers and pitchers who end up in a poor fielding position on the follow-through.

With runners on first or second base, a successful sacrifice bunt will advance the runners into scoring position. As the pitcher starts the windup, the batter squares around either by moving the back foot up nearly parallel with the front foot or by pivoting on the heel of the front foot and the toe of the back foot.

The bat is held level or at a 45-degree angle (the 45-degree technique is harder to master). The knees bend, and the weight is forward to prevent lunging. The upper hand slides 12 inches up the bat, and the bottom hand stays on the handle. Players should grip the bat lightly with the upper hand, keeping the fingers underneath and the thumb on top in the form of a V. Figure 8.37 shows the progression from a normal stance to squaring away and bunting.

From the start of the pitcher's delivery to the actual contact of ball with bat, the player must focus on the ball. The hitter's arms are extended

Figure 8.37   Progression to bunt.

to position the bat at the top of the strike zone, covering the entire plate. Letting the ball come to the bat, the batter gives with the arms and hands as the ball is met, "catching" the ball as if the end of the bat were a glove.

Keeping the bat above the ball will prevent popping up, which is the worst thing a batter can do when sacrifice bunting. The batter should also avoid bunting back to the pitcher or hitting the ball hard, because the defense could turn a double play or get the lead runner. Ideally, the player places the sacrifice bunt down the third-base line. For a right-handed batter to do this, the player must bring the handle close to the body with the bottom hand. To bunt down the first-base line, the player must push out the handle with the bottom hand.

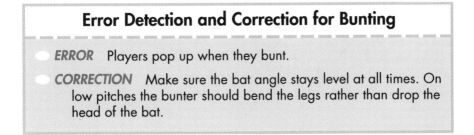

Error Detection and Correction for Bunting

ERROR   Players pop up when they bunt.

CORRECTION   Make sure the bat angle stays level at all times. On low pitches the bunter should bend the legs rather than drop the head of the bat.

Bunting Game

SQUEEZE PLAY

Goal

To practice defending the sacrifice bunt with runners on first and third bases

Description

Play 6v6. Assign a complete infield and place runners on first and third bases (see figure 8.38). The pitcher should pitch a ball so the batter can bunt it. The runners cannot leave their bases until the ball reaches home plate, but the runner on third must attempt to score. The defense attempts to throw the runner out at home plate or force the runner at second base.

Award three points to the defense if the runner is out at home, two points if the runner is out at second, and one point if the runner is out at first. Switch teams after everyone on the offensive side has bunted.

To make the game easier

⊙ Place a runner on first base only.

⊙ Keep runners on first and third, but the runner on third doesn't have to try to score.

To make the game harder

⊙ Allow the runners to leave their bases with the pitch.

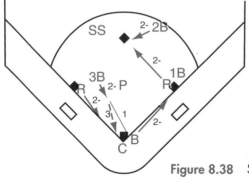

Figure 8.38 Set-up for Squeeze Play.

Baserunning

The last thing you want to do on the bases is to waste scoring opportunities. So stress baserunning at every practice. Baserunners must always know where the ball is, how many outs there are, and what they will do when the ball is hit. They must also pick up signals given by coaches. Teach your players to be heads-up, aggressive baserunners.

Before you can teach players how to run the bases, however, they first must know how to run. Teach them proper sprinting form: head up, body leaning forward, on the toes, high knee lift, and arms pumping front to back (not across the body; see figure 8.39).

Running to First Base

When a hitter makes contact, he or she should drop the bat at the end of the swing, then move quickly and efficiently out of the batter's box. The player turns in the direction of first base, stays low, drives out of the box, and starts down the line with a jab step of the back foot.

The run to first base should be an all-out sprint, and the player should run "through" the bag, like a sprinter hitting a finish-line tape. Tell your players not to lunge or jump at the bag because that is not as fast as a running step. Make sure your players are ready to advance to second if the throw to first is a bad one.

If the player gets a hit into the outfield, she or he should "think second" by running a flat arc to first base and continuing hard past the

Figure 8.39 The proper baserunning technique.

bag, looking for an opportunity to advance to second. The runner begins the flat arc about 6 feet out of the batter's box, curving no more than 3 feet outside the line, and hits the left inside corner of the base with the left foot. On extra base hits, baserunners should continue the pattern of flat arcs to each base (see figure 8.40).

If a baserunner takes the turn at first, instruct him or her to sprint about a third of the distance to second base. The player will know by the first-base coach's commands whether to go to second or return to first.

When the pitcher's body motion indicates the start of the pitch, the runner takes a quick crossover step to initiate the attempted steal. Getting that split-second jump on the pitcher is often the difference between being out or safe at second base.

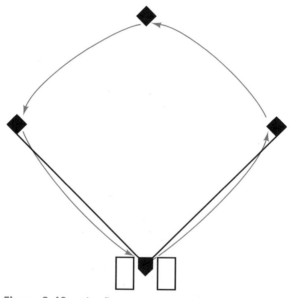

Figure 8.40   The flat arc.

Sliding

When approaching a base, a player must decide in an instant whether or not to slide. If the play at the base appears close or if a coach or teammate is yelling to get down, the player should slide. Once the decision is made, it should be carried out. Players often change their minds at the last second, which increases the chance of injury. However, most injuries result from poor sliding technique. Teach your players how to slide safely and correctly, and give them plenty of opportunities to practice so they become comfortable with the actual correct motion.

Here is the sequence of the bent-leg slide you should teach players:

1. Start the slide 10 to 12 feet from the bag.
2. Don't drop down to the ground—slide to the bag.
3. As you approach the bag, bend your knees (which will drop your hips). Then extend your right leg toward the bag and bend your left leg under your right knee to form a "4" (see figure 8.41).
4. Slide on your buttocks, not on your side or hips.
5. Tuck chin to chest to prevent banging your head.
6. Your extended foot should be 6 to 8 inches off the ground to slide over the bag.
7. Keep your hands up; don't drag them across the ground as you slide.

Figure 8.41   In the bent-leg slide, legs form a "4."

Error Detection and Correction for Sliding

ERROR   Players keep jamming their ankles into the bag.

CORRECTION   Designate a spot at which players should start their slide—about 10 to 12 feet before the bag. Teach players to run hard and try to extend their slides across the top of the ground.

Tagging Up

When a ball is hit in the air, the runner must decide whether to go halfway to the next base or to tag up (remain in contact with the base during the fly ball, with the intention of advancing to the next base after the ball is caught). The first- or third-base coach can help make the call. There's no decision to make on foul fly balls: The runner should always tag up. Outfield flies are tougher, requiring a quick assessment of how deep the ball is hit, the positioning of the outfield, and the throwing arm of the outfielder who is likely to make the catch. Tell your runners that, in most situations, they should play it safe and not try to advance, unless a coach tells them to do so (though it doesn't hurt to force a hard throw to the next base by bluffing a run; the hurried throw could be off-line). If a runner is going to tag up, she or he needs to stay low, keep the knees bent, and push hard off the bag on the coach's command to "Go!"

Defensive Skills

Individual defensive skills include throwing, pitching, and catching (including catching pitches and throws, fielding grounders, and catching fly balls). The team with the best hitters won't necessarily win the game if their pitching is weak and their defense is poor. Especially in youth competition, teams with strong pitching and defense have a leg up on victory—it is for these reasons that we have emphasized learning defensive skills in the season plans.

Throwing

Throwing is one of the most important skills in softball. Stress to your players that accuracy is more important than speed. Many players throw wildly in their attempts to put some zip on the ball.

Teach your players to throw over the top (overhand) and not sidearm. Throwing the ball over the top will give players greater control and accuracy. Conversely, throwing sidearm can lead to bad throwing habits, wildness, and undue strain on young elbows.

Overhand Throw

A player's throwing motion is like a set of fingerprints: Everyone has one, but it's slightly different from anyone else's. However, to throw a softball well, every player must use some type of grip, windup, delivery, and follow-through. Here is the overhand throwing technique to teach your players.

○ **Grip.** The player should grip the ball in the throwing hand.

○ **Windup.** Bringing the throwing arm back and up, the player turns so the front shoulder is pointed at the target. At this point, the weight is on the back foot. The glove hand points toward the target. The arm extends behind the body with wrist cocked and elbow bent (see figure 8.42a).

○ **Delivery.** Now the player picks up the lead foot and strides toward the target. As the lead foot touches the ground, the hips are turned so that the throwing-side hip drives toward the target (see figure 8.42b). The player transfers weight from the back foot to the front foot and brings the throwing arm forward just before releasing the ball. Encourage players to look at the target when throwing.

○ **Follow-Through.** The player points the throwing hand at the target and swings the back leg around. The follow-through ends with the throwing arm down in the front of the body and the feet almost parallel, in a balanced ready position (see figure 8.42c).

a   b   c

Figure 8.42   The steps of the overhand throw.

Error Detection and Correction for Overhand Throws

● *ERROR* Players rush their throws after fielding the ball, which causes them to miss their targets.

● *CORRECTION* Remind players that they must first field the ball properly, then pick the ball from their glove, set their feet, and use good mechanics for the grip, windup, delivery, and follow-through.

Sidearm and Three-Quarter-Arm Throws

Although you may teach the proper overhand throwing technique to all your players, count on having to correct them for dropping the arm in delivery. Many players use the three-quarter-arm throw, but it is often the sign of a tired arm. A player should use the sidearm throw only when there is no other choice or when throwing to a base from a short distance. Improper throwing technique at an early age can lead to bad throwing habits and injury later in a player's career.

The best way to monitor throwing technique is to watch players during warm-up. If you see them using improper mechanics or lapsing into a three-quarter-arm or sidearm motion, immediately show them the correct grip, windup, delivery, and follow-through of the overhand throwing technique.

Snap Throw

A better choice than the sidearm or three-quarter-arm throw for close distances is the snap throw. Like the overhand throw, it can be taught in a simple progression:

1. Facing a partner, the player brings the ball up to the ear with the arm bent (see figure 8.43a).

2. The player extends the throwing arm toward the person receiving the ball, aiming to hit the player in the chest (see figure 8.43b).

3. The thrower's arm should be parallel to the ground after the follow-through, with the hand and fingers pointed toward the target (see figure 8.43c).

Figure 8.43   The steps of the snap throw.

Make sure that the hand and the arm go straight toward the partner. If the player brings the throwing arm across the body or follows through past a point parallel to the ground, the ball will go wide of the target or too low. At higher levels, this is the throw used in rundowns, so it is important that players learn from the beginning to be accurate with their throws.

Error Detection and Correction for Snap Throws

● *ERROR*   Players make poor short throws, either too low or off to one side.

● *CORRECTION*   Remind players to stop the throwing arm at the point perpendicular to the ground when initiating the delivery (see figure 8.43 on page 129). On the follow-through, players must throw directly at the target and not across the body.

Crow Hop

Because of the distances involved in most throws from the outfield, an outfielder needs to learn a *crow hop*, a move that uses the body to provide additional power in the throw. Many players throw strictly with the arm, which greatly restricts how far they can throw and leads to arm injuries. The fundamentals are basically the same as for the overhand throw except the hop allows the outfielder to quickly shift the weight back and gather momentum in order to use the body as well as the arm in the throw.

As the fielder catches the ball, he or she steps forward with the ball-side, or back, leg (right leg for a right-handed thrower).

The player skips on the ball-side foot (right foot for a right-handed thrower), rotating the shoulders so that the glove-side shoulder (left shoulder for a right-handed thrower) is now pointed toward the target (see figure 8.44a). Maintaining weight on the back leg, the player extends the throwing arm back (see figure 8.44b).

The player executes the throw, shifting the weight forward to the front foot (see figure 8.44c). The player's shoulders rotate back square to the target, allowing the throwing arm to come through with the throwing hand ending down by the glove-side knee. The back leg should always step toward the target.

a   *b*   *c*

Figure 8.44   The steps of the crow hop.

Throwing Game

MAKING THE PLAY

Goal

To make an accurate throw to the appropriate base

Description

Play 6v6. Field an entire infield. Offensive runners rotate in as needed. You will hit ground balls to the fielders, who must field the ball and make the appropriate throw.

Throws to first—Hit one ground ball to each fielder (including a bunt for the catcher). Each fielder must field and throw to first. A runner at home runs to first on contact and tries to beat the throw (see figure 8.45a). On the ball hit to the first-base player, the pitcher must cover first. A perfect score is six points (six outs recorded).

Throws to second—Hit one ground ball to each fielder (including a bunt for the catcher). Each fielder must field and throw to second (see figure 8.45b). A runner at first runs to second on contact and tries to beat the throw. A perfect score is six points (six outs recorded).

Throws to home—Hit one ground ball to each infielder (except the catcher). Each fielder must field and throw home (see figure 8.45c). A

(continued)

Making the Play *(continued)*

runner at third runs home on contact and tries to beat the throw. A perfect score is five points (five outs recorded).

Keep track of points and rotate offense and defense after these three sets of plays.

To make the game easier

○ Hit easy grounders directly to the players.

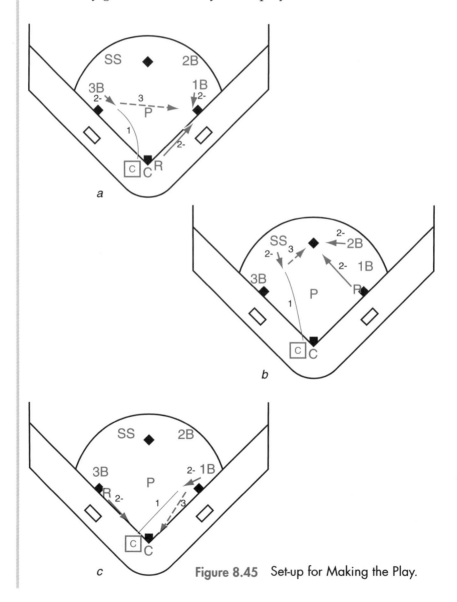

Figure 8.45 Set-up for Making the Play.

To make the game harder
- Hit harder ground balls.
- Hit ground balls that force the fielders to move one direction or another.

Pitching

In softball, the pitcher uses an underhand motion to throw the ball. In fast-pitch, speed, movement, and location are the keys to pitching success. In slow-pitch, arc and location are most important.

In fast-pitch, a team's success is often determined by the performance of its pitcher, so the position deserves considerable attention. Fast-pitching is a specialized skill, requiring specialized instruction. If you are a beginning coach, try to find an experienced pitching coach to work with the pitchers on your team. Also, read books on pitching and attend clinics to become a better coach for your pitchers.

Slow-pitching, although not as mechanically complex, requires excellent control. Nothing is worse than playing the field or watching when a slow-pitch pitcher can't find the plate. So you must work with your pitchers to develop their accuracy.

Maintaining Balance

One of the most crucial points in the fast-pitch delivery is the *balance point*. That is where the throwing hand is at its highest point above the head and the glove-side foot is at its highest point above the ground (see figure 8.46). This is a critical point in the delivery. Failure to keep the weight back means the weight is shifted forward too soon, forcing the pitcher to throw with just the arm. Trying to generate power or speed too early in the delivery often leads to this problem. The signs of transferring weight too early are overstriding, putting weight on the front foot only, and moving the head and shoulders forward ahead of the hips and hand.

Shoulder Position

Young pitchers often err by pitching with the shoulder instead of the wrist, leading the action forward with the throwing-arm shoulder as the arm begins the downward swing from the balance point. The hand *with* the ball should always lead the action.

Wrist-Hand Position

A strong wrist snap is crucial for creating speed and movement on the ball. The pitcher must cock the wrist on the downward swing and then snap it at the power point by the hip, as in figure 8.47. With the fast ball,

Figure 8.46 Balance point in softball delivery.

Figure 8.47 The wrist snap in softball pitching.

the palm and the middle finger point directly at home plate; the first and second fingers are the last to come off the ball.

Hip Position

The hips, which act as a coil, first store power and then release it just as the hand hits the power point (see figure 8.48). A common error is for the pitcher to close the hips toward home before the hand reaches the power point, forcing the hand to go around the hip instead of driving down and through directly toward home plate. Remind your pitchers that they cannot pitch through the hip to the release point. After delivering the pitch, your pitcher needs to bring the ball-side leg toward the plate and assume a fielding position in case the ball is hit back at her or him.

Fast-Pitching Fundamentals

Keep in mind these points when teaching the fast pitch.

1. The ball is held with the fingers, not in the hand.
2. The grip should be firm but not tight.
3. The pre-motion is a natural start to prepare for the pitching delivery. It is a controlled motion, and the body does not start the delivery or go forward until this motion is completed.

Figure 8.48   Proper hip position.

4. The arm acts like a whip and should be relaxed throughout the motion.

5. A pitcher needs maximum acceleration on the downward swing with complete arm extension for leverage and rotation in a smooth plane parallel to the body.

6. The stride of the glove-side foot should be thought of as a step, not a lunge or a falling action. It is a controlled movement.

7. The step should be straight toward home plate, with the foot landing at no more than a 45-degree angle to home.

8. The stride should be long enough to maintain the pitcher's balance and allow for sufficient weight transfer.

9. The weight must be kept back until that explosive movement when the ball is snapped and all the power resources are thrust forward.

Slow-Pitching Fundamentals

The mechanics of delivering a slow pitch are much the same as those described for a fast pitch. However, you should note these important differences:

1. The throwing arm motion is not whiplike but rather an easy, semi-circle movement (see figure 8.49).

Figure 8.49   Half-circle motion.

2. The weight transfer to the front foot is gradual, not explosive.
3. The ball is released in front of the body and tossed upward, unlike hip-released bullets in fast-pitch (see figure 8.50).
4. The wrist helps in the throwing motion, but it is not snapped quickly as it is in fast-pitch.
5. Immediately after the follow-through, the pitcher takes several steps back for protection and fielding purposes.

Figure 8.50   Releasing ball in front of body.

Error Detection and Correction for the Balance Point

● *ERROR* The pitcher can't get any speed on the ball, even though she or he has a strong arm.

● *CORRECTION* Have the pitcher start the delivery and then stop at the balance point. The weight should remain back. Check the pitcher's stride to make sure it is not too long (the glove-side leg should be just slightly ahead of the pitcher's body at the release point).

Pitching Game

BULLS-EYE!

Goal

To throw strikes

Description

Split your pitchers into two teams. You'll also need two catchers (see figure 8.51). You and an assistant or another player will call balls and strikes. The two teams throw to their catchers at the same time to keep the game moving. Each pitcher throws five pitches, then gives way to the next pitcher. They repeat this so that each pitcher throws 10 pitches. The team with the highest number of strikes wins.

Figure 8.51 Set-up for Bulls-Eye!

To make the game easier
  ⊙ Shorten the pitching distance.

To make the game harder
  ⊙ Make pitchers throw strikes to certain locations (e.g., low and to one side of the plate).

Catching

Another major defensive skill is catching. This includes catching pitches, catching thrown balls, fielding ground balls, catching fly balls, and catching line drives. It is a fundamental defensive skill; both fly-outs and ground-outs begin and end with catches. And the player who has to catch the most balls is, appropriately enough, the catcher.

Catching Pitched Balls

The catcher's position is the most demanding in fast-pitch softball. During a game, the catcher is the busiest player on the field—crouching behind the plate, calling pitches, blocking balls, keeping track of the count on each batter, repositioning teammates defensively, and so on. So select a sturdy, smart, and strong youngster to be your catcher.

A catcher's mitt is padded and rounded so that the ball easily lands in the pocket. The extra padding also helps ensure the safety of the player using the glove.

Basic Position. The catcher assumes a comfortable crouching position about two feet behind the plate. The catcher uses her or his glove to give the pitcher a throwing target (see figure 8.52). The catcher can move the body and the target around the plate to give the pitcher an inside or outside target. Have catchers protect the throwing hand from foul-tipped balls by placing it behind the back of the leg.

With the legs shoulder-width apart, the catcher keeps the weight on the balls of the feet so he or she is ready to move in any direction for a poorly thrown ball. Staying low helps the catcher avoid being hit by the swing of the batter and allows the umpire to see the ball as it crosses the plate.

When a ball is pitched in the dirt, the catcher should try to block the ball and keep it in front of the body. For example, if a ball is thrown in the dirt to the catcher's right, she or he steps out with the right leg, dropping to both knees and keeping the ball in the center of the body. The catcher's left leg drags behind while the glove moves between the

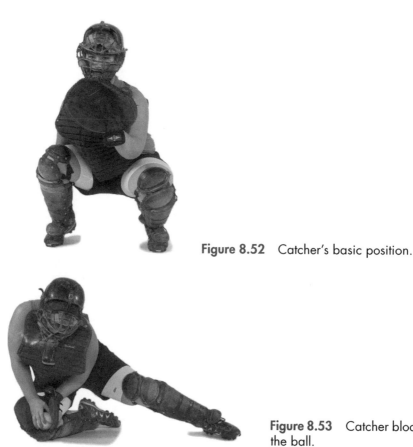

Figure 8.52   Catcher's basic position.

Figure 8.53   Catcher blocking the ball.

legs, as shown in figure 8.53. The catcher makes the same movements on pitches thrown in the dirt to the left side.

When a pitch is thrown in the dirt just in front of the catcher, he or she drops both knees to the ground and slides into the ball. With the back side of the glove on the ground, the catcher places the glove between the legs to execute the block. Bowing the back and bringing the chin down to the chest protects the throat area and helps the catcher keep the eyes on the ball.

Up Position.   With runners on base, your catcher should be in the up position: feet shoulder-width apart and the right foot slightly in front of the left. The catcher should extend the glove hand away from the body, providing a large target. He or she should keep the back almost parallel to the ground (see figure 8.54). This position will allow your catcher to receive the pitch and throw to a base quickly.

When a runner attempts a steal, the catcher should lean into the ball just before catching it, making sure not to come forward too soon, which could lead to an interference call if the batter swings and hits the catcher.

While catching the ball, the catcher should quickly move the glove-side leg forward into the throwing position (jump turn), rotate the shoulders to be parallel to the batter's box, and bring the glove hand near the ear, where it should meet the throwing hand (see figure 8.55). The catcher

Figure 8.54 Catcher in up position.

Figure 8.55 Catcher getting into throwing position.

makes the throw by transferring weight from the back leg to the front leg, staying low, rotating the shoulders, and following through (see figure 8.56). The follow-through involves bringing the throwing hand to the opposite knee while stepping toward the base being thrown to with the throwing-side leg.

Figure 8.56   Catcher throwing.

Catching Game

BACKSTOP

Goal

To execute the skills needed to be a catcher

Description

You need four people for this game—a pitcher (which could be you), a catcher, a runner, and a fielder. This game highlights five skills required of a catcher. You can split any one of the following skills into a separate game, or you can do all five in one.

Blocking pitches—Throw three wild pitches in the dirt in front of the catcher (see figure 8.57a). The pitch must be within reach of the catcher (not too far to the side or over the catcher's head). The catcher

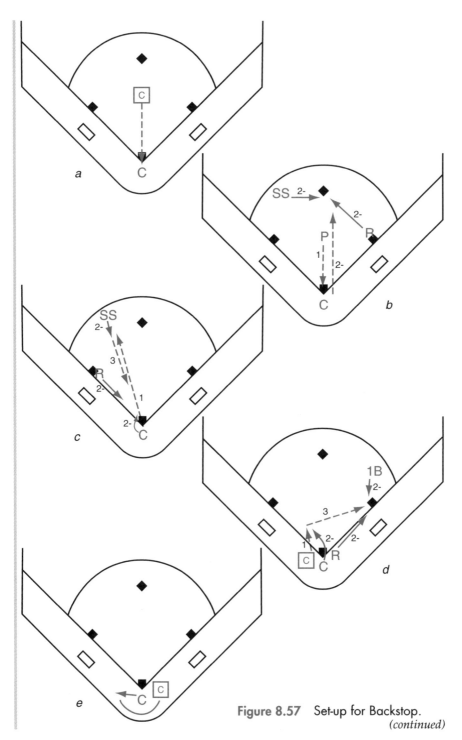

Figure 8.57 Set-up for Backstop.
(continued)

Backstop *(continued)*

attempts to block each pitch. Catcher scores one point for each successful block.

Throwing out runners—The fielder plays shortstop. A runner on first tries to steal second as the pitcher pitches. The catcher throws to the shortstop covering second, who tries to tag the runner out (see figure 8.57b). Do this play three times. The catcher scores one point for each throw to second that arrives in time to get the runner out (the point is scored even if the shortstop drops the ball at second or misses the tag).

Blocking the plate—The runner is on third base. The catcher (or you) throws a ground ball to the fielder, who is playing shortstop (see figure 8.57c). The runner breaks for home and tries to score. The catcher blocks the plate and attempts to tag out the runner. Do this play three times, scoring one point for each successful tag.

Fielding a bunt and throwing to first base—A runner is at home and the fielder is at first base (see figure 8.57d). Roll a bunt down the first- or third-base line; the runner heads for first base as the ball leaves your hand. The catcher, starting from a crouched position, springs up as the ball is rolled and the runner takes off for first. The catcher attempts to throw the runner out. Do this play three times, scoring a point for the catcher for each out at first (if the ball arrives in time to get the runner out, score the point for the catcher even if the fielder at first base drops the ball).

Catching a foul pop—Hit or throw high foul pops near home plate (see figure 8.57e). The catcher, starting from a crouched position and with a mask on, tracks the pop-up, discards the mask, and attempts to catch the ball. Do this play three times, scoring a point for each caught pop-up.

Catching Thrown Balls

A fielder may receive a ball when covering a base or not covering a base. Many of the same principles apply in either case. First we'll address catching principles in general, and then we'll look at covering a base.

General Principles. To catch a thrown ball, the player should position the glove according to the flight of the ball. If the ball is below the waist, the fingers and the palm of the glove hand should be pointed down with the mitt fully open (see figure 8.58a). If the ball is chest-high, the fingers and the palm of the glove should be pointing out, with the thumbs pointing to the sky (see figure 8.58b). If the ball is above the chest, the fingers should point toward the sky (see figure 8.58c).

Figure 8.58 Proper technique for catching a ball *(a)* below the waist, *(b)* chest-high, and *(c)* above the chest.

In all catching attempts, players should

1. keep their eyes on the ball;
2. have both hands ready, with arms relaxed and extended toward the ball (see figure 8.59);
3. bend the elbows to absorb the force of the throw; and
4. watch the ball into the glove and squeeze it (see figure 8.60).

After the catch, the player should immediately grip the ball with the throwing hand in the correct overhand throwing technique.

Figure 8.59 Preparing to catch.

Figure 8.60   Fielder gripping ball with glove.

Covering a Base. When accepting a throw at a base, an infielder needs to sprint to the bag and get in position to receive the ball in the middle of the body. The fielder should face the thrower, bend the knees, and have the legs slightly more than shoulder-width apart for a good base of support (see figure 8.61).

As with catching a thrown ball anywhere, the player should fully extend the glove arm, keep the head still, and watch the ball into the glove, giving with the ball as it enters the glove.

On force-outs, players shouldn't commit a foot to the bag too early (see figure 8.62). If the throw is off target, it is harder to adjust to the

Figure 8.61   Covering a base.

Figure 8.62   Player doesn't commit to bag too early.

throw. Players should keep their foot on the side of the bag rather than on top; the latter invites injury.

Here are the keys for two types of base coverage, the first-base player covering first and the pitcher covering first. The pitcher has to cover first base on balls hit to the first-base player or on balls that pull the first-base player far enough off the bag that he or she can't retreat to the base in time to receive a throw from the second-base player. Pitchers should move toward first to cover the base on balls hit to the right side of the infield.

First-base player covering first

⊙ Sprint to the bag when the ground ball is hit.

⊙ Face the thrower.

⊙ Touch the bag with the throwing-side heel, bending the knees.

⊙ If the ball can be caught in the air, wait until the last possible moment, plant a foot on the inside of the bag, and stretch to meet the ball (in other words, don't commit to the bag too early).

⊙ Come off the bag in position to throw, if appropriate.

Pitcher covering first

⊙ Break toward first on a ball hit to the right side of the infield.

◎ Run diagonally toward the first-base line, then run parallel with the baseline once you're within a few feet of the line.

◎ Focus on the base and the ball. As you near the base, the focus should be on the ball.

◎ Extend your glove, giving the fielder a good target.

◎ Catch the ball and step on the nearest inside portion of the base.

Error Detection and Correction for Catching Balls at First Base

ERROR The first-base player has trouble catching high, but not bad, throws.

CORRECTION Encourage the player to wait longer before stretching out and shift the weight off the heels in case he or she needs to jump. As the throw approaches, then the first-base player extends upward for the catch.

Fielding Ground Balls

Now let's look at how you can instruct players to catch ground balls. Emphasize these five components of the skill: assume ready position, move to the ball, field, skip-and-throw, and follow-through.

Assume Ready Position. To assume the ready position, your players should have their feet slightly wider apart than the shoulders, their knees bent, and their weight over the balls of their feet (see figure 8.63). The hands hang low between the legs, with the glove open wide. From

Figure 8.63   Ready position for ground balls.

this ready position, the player can get a good jump on the ball and move quickly in the direction it is hit.

Move to the Ball. When a ground ball is hit in the direction of an infielder, the player moves to position his or her body in front of the ball. Teach your players always to lead with the glove, no matter which direction they move. This will help them stay low to the ground, the correct position for fielding a ball. Infielders should judge the speed and spin of the ball to determine where they need to move for good fielding position. With practice, players will learn to "pick a hop," or anticipate where the ball will bounce nearest to them and then move there to catch the ball. It's best to stay low and catch the ball on a low hop near the glove rather than on an "in-between hop" a few to several feet in front of the glove. In-between hops are much harder to gauge and fielders are much more likely to make an error on them. Therefore, fielders will need to learn to charge the ball—move toward it— to get that low hop. In this way they actively "play the ball" rather than letting it play them. It's much easier to field a ball when moving toward it than when rocking back on the heels and moving away from it.

Field. Here are the steps for teaching your players the proper fielding position for ground balls:

1. Bend your knees and keep the glove open.
2. Extend your arms in front of your body and reach out for the ball. The glove-side foot is forward.
3. Watch the ball all the way into the glove and trap it with your throwing hand (see figure 8.64a).
4. Keep the backside low and field the ball in the middle of your body, cushioning it with "soft" hands into the body to the belt area.

Skip-and-Throw. The skip-and-throw technique will help your infielders get rid of the ball quickly after they've fielded it. While cushioning the ball into the glove, the infielder lines up the glove-side shoulder and hip with the throwing target. With eyes focused on the target and the glove in the center of the chest, the player skips forward and prepares to throw (see figure 8.64b). As the throwing hand leaves the glove, the arm extends down and back in a comfortable, relaxed position (see figure 8.64c). Pushing off the back leg, the player then throws over the top, moving the throwing shoulder and arm forward quickly (see figure 8.64d). A strong wrist snap at the point of release will result in better accuracy.

Follow-Through. During the follow-through, the player points the throwing-side shoulder toward the target and lifts the back leg off the ground. The player's momentum should be forward, in the direction of the throw (see figure 8.64e).

a   *b*   *c*

d   *e*

Figure 8.64   Steps for fielding ground balls.

Error Detection and Correction for Fielding Ground Balls

● *ERROR*   Players misfield the ball when they have to field it on the run.

● *CORRECTION*

1. Tell players to concentrate on the ball as they move toward it.

2. Instruct them to keep the seat and hands low and the hands in front of the body.

3. Remind players to watch the ball into the glove.

4. Emphasize that players should cushion the ball to the belt area by pulling the arms in toward the midsection.

Fielding Ground Balls Game

AIRTIGHT D

Goal

To field grounders and throw to the appropriate base

Description

Play 5v5. On defense, have a pitcher and players at first, second, third, and shortstop (see figure 8.65). Rotate the five offensive players in as runners (sometimes you'll need more than one runner). Complete these plays in sequence:

1. No runners on base. A runner is at home, ready to run to first. Hit a ground ball to a fielder (you choose, but don't tell the fielders where you're hitting it). The fielder tries to throw the runner out at first (see figure 8.65a).

2. Runner on first. A runner is at home, ready to run to first. Hit a ground ball to a fielder, who makes the appropriate play (preferably to second base to get the lead runner, but depending on the hit, the throw might need to go to first base; see figure 8.65b).

3. Runner on second. A runner is at home, ready to run to first. Hit a ground ball to a fielder, who attempts to hold the runner to

(continued)

Airtight D *(continued)*

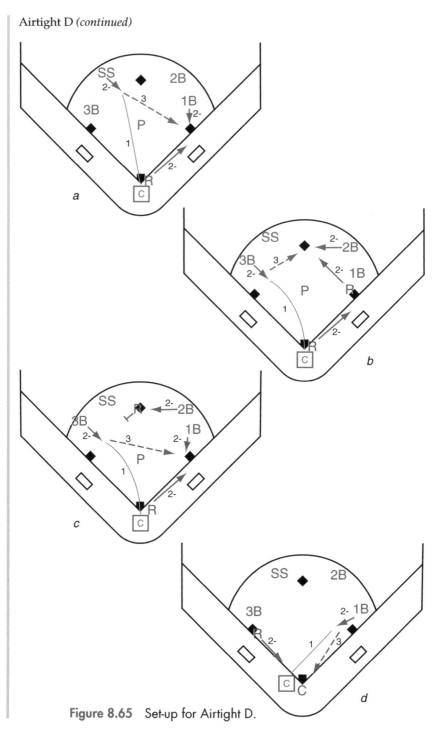

Figure 8.65   Set-up for Airtight D.

second and throw the runner out at first (or throw the runner out at third if he or she attempts to go; see figure 8.65c).

4. Runner on third. A runner is at home, ready to run to first. Infield is in for the play at the plate (see figure 8.65d). Hit a ground ball to a fielder, who must make the appropriate play—throwing home to get the runner or holding the runner at third and throwing to first (or throwing to first if there is no chance to get the runner going home).

Perform this cycle of plays three times with the same defense in the field. Alternate your hits so that all the players get about an equal amount of plays to make. The defense scores a point for every out recorded—unless you judge that the fielder should have tried for an out at second, third, or home rather than throwing to first.

After three cycles, switch the offensive and defensive teams and perform the cycles three more times.

To make the game easier

⊙ Use fewer cycles.
⊙ Use no baserunners.

To make the game harder

⊙ Hit balls that are harder to make plays on.

Catching Fly Balls

Sound team defense includes a core of capable outfielders. Developing good skills in the outfield requires diligent practice.

Like their teammates in the infield, outfielders must be in the ready position and prepared for action on each pitch. It's easy for players to lose concentration in the outfield because they're so far away from most of the action. It's your job to convince your outfielders that they must be alert: knees slightly bent, feet squared and facing home plate, weight on the balls of the feet, and gloves waist-high (see figure 8.66).

Softball is a game of quick action and reaction. Defensive players must move to the ball at full speed. Most young athletes tend to drift to the ball, which means they arrive at the point of contact just as the ball does, instead of earlier.

Teach players these tips for catching fly balls properly once they have run to them:

⊙ Keep your eyes on the ball at all times.
⊙ Whenever possible, position yourself behind the ball.

Figure 8.66   Ready position for an outfielder.

- Run with the glove down, in a typical sprinting position.
- Communicate by shouting, "Mine!" or, "I've got it!" at least twice.
- Keep your hands down until in position to make the catch.
- Catch the ball in front of your head, using two hands if possible, with your arms almost fully extended.
- As the catch is made, give with the impact by bringing the glove down and in toward your chest.
- Always get back quickly on a ball hit over your head. Keep the ball in front of you.

A good throw from the outfield finishes a strong defensive play. After catching the ball with two hands, the player makes a crow hop forward to distribute the weight on the back leg (see "Crow Hop" on page 130). As she or he lines up the hip, shoulder, and glove with the target (second base, third base, or home plate), the arm extends loosely behind. The player's weight comes forward, and the player pushes hard off the throwing-side leg while releasing the ball from an overhand position. The momentum of the throw brings the back leg off the ground, and the player continues to move forward after the throw. Accurate, low, one-bounce throws are best. See the "Relays and Cutoffs" section on pages 91-95.

Catching Fly Balls Game

ON THE FLY

Goal

To catch fly balls and throw the ball to the appropriate base

Description

Play 6v6. The defense has three outfielders, two infielders (who will play different positions depending on the play), and a catcher. The offense rotates runners in as needed. Alternate hitting or throwing fly balls to the three outfielders, who must catch the ball and make the appropriate play in each of these situations:

- Runner on first, none out. Infielders are at second and short (see figure 8.67a).
- Runner on second, none out. Infielders are at second or short and third (see figure 8.67b).
- Runner on third, none out. Infielders are at second or short and third (see figure 8.67c).
- Runners on first and second, none out. Infielders are at second or short and third (see figure 8.67d).
- Runners on second and third, none out. Infielders are at second or short and third (see figure 8.67e).

(For plays to right field, use a second-base player; for plays to center or left, use a shortstop.)

Each outfielder gets a fly ball for each situation. Runners tag up and advance at their own risk. The defense gets one point for every out—whether by fly balls caught or baserunners put out. Subtract a point from the defense if one or more baserunners advance on the play. Keep track of points; switch offense and defense after each outfielder has had five catchable fly balls.

To make the game easier

- Throw or hit shallower fly balls.
- Throw or hit fly balls directly at the outfielders.

(continued)

On the Fly *(continued)*

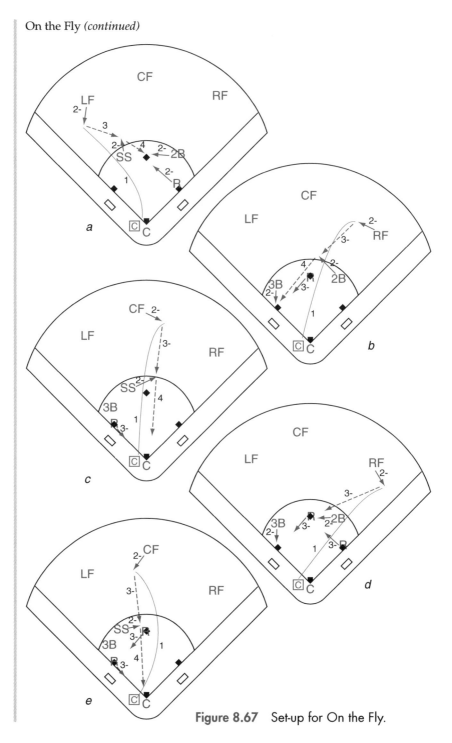

Figure 8.67 Set-up for On the Fly.

To make the game harder
- Throw or hit deeper fly balls.
- Throw or hit fly balls that make the outfielders move.

Catching Line Drives

A line drive is a hard hit that moves directly in a line low to the ground (usually at the height of the player or lower). Teach your players to try to catch line drives above the waist, if possible. They can do this by crouching down. That way, if they try to catch the ball with the glove fingers up and the ball pops out, they still have the ability to quickly turn the glove over and get the dropped ball.

chapter 9

Season Plans

We hope you have learned a lot from this book: what your responsibilities are as a coach, how to communicate well and provide for safety, how to use the games approach to teach and shape skills, and how to coach on game days. But game days make up only a portion of your season—you and your players will spend more time in practice than in competition. How well you conduct practices and prepare your players for competition significantly affects both your and your players' enjoyment and success throughout the season.

In this chapter, then, we present three season plans: one for 8- to 9-year-olds, one for 10- to 11-year-olds, and one for 12- to 14-year-olds. Use these plans as guidelines for conducting your practices. These plans are not the *only* way to approach your season, but they do present an appropriate teaching progression. Remember to incorporate the games approach as you use these plans.

The season plans have two components: the first is purpose and the second is tactics and skills. By *purpose* we mean the overarching objective of the particular practice—the main focus of that practice. *Tactics and skills* refer to the specifics you will be teaching or refining during a practice in order to meet the purpose.

Good luck and good coaching!

Season Plan for 8- to 9-Year-Olds

Many 8- to 9-year-olds have had little or no exposure to softball. Don't assume they have any knowledge of the game. Help them explore the basic tactics and skills of the sport, as suggested in the following season plan.

Practice	Purpose	Tactics and skills
1	To learn throwing and catching techniques	Proper grip; throwing; catching; throwing to bases
2	To defend in the infield on ground balls	Fielding grounders and throwing to first base; hitting and running to first base
3	To learn hitting mechanics	Hitting off a batting tee; fielding batted balls; running to first base after hitting
4	To defend in the outfield on fly balls and ground balls	Fielding grounders and throwing to the appropriate base; fielding fly balls and throwing to the appropriate base; hitting off the tee and fielding the hits
5	To develop bunting techniques and baserunning skills	Bunting and running to first base; fielding bunts and throwing to first base
6	To work on hitting and baserunning mechanics	Hitting off the batting tee; running the bases; tagging up and advancing; fielding and throwing

7	To defend at second base by using force plays	Fielding ground balls; making force plays at second base
8	To work on pitching and throwing mechanics	Pitching; hitting; throwing; running out the hits
9	To defend at third base by fielding bunts and making tag plays	Making tag plays at third base; fielding bunts; baserunning
10	To work on hitting and baserunning strategies	Hitting off the batting tee; fielding and throwing to bases; running out the hits
11	To defend in the outfield, including making relay throws	Fielding ground balls and fly balls in the outfield; throwing to a relay person; running the bases
12	To work on bat control and hitting mechanics	Hitting off the batting tee; hitting only ground balls; running the bases
13	To develop pitching and bunting	Pitching; bunting; running out bunts
14	To defend at second base and first base by converting double plays	Fielding grounders and throwing to second base; running the bases; making double plays

Season Plan for 10- to 11-Year-Olds

This season plan builds on the previous one as players practice the fundamental tactics and skills and add a few new strategies, including defending in rundowns, defending home on balls hit to the infield, and executing the hit-and-run.

Practice	Purpose	Tactics and skills
1	To learn throwing, catching, and fielding ground balls	Throwing; fielding ground balls; throwing to the appropriate base

2	To develop hitting techniques	Hitting off a batting tee; running to first base; fielding and throwing
3	To learn pitching mechanics	Pitching to each other; pitching to a batter; hitting and baserunning
4	To defend second base on force plays	Fielding grounders and throwing to second base; covering second base; running from first to second base
5	To defend second base and first base on double plays	Making double plays; trying to break up double plays
6	To learn bunting techniques and baserunning skills	Bunting; fielding bunts; baserunning; throwing to the right base; covering bases
7	To defend third base in tag and force play situations	Covering third base in force situations; catching fly balls in the outfield; tagging up and running from second to third base
8	To improve batting techniques and speed of the swing	Hitting off a tee to the follow-through side of the field; baserunning; hitting against the coach's pitching
9	To learn cutoff strategies and defend against balls hit to the outfield with a runner on first base	Fielding balls; backing up the outfielders; throwing to the cutoff player; covering bases; baserunning
10	To defend against balls hit to the outfield with a runner on third base	Fielding fly balls in the outfield; tagging up on third base; throwing to the cutoff person; improving throwing speed and release
11	To work on baserunning techniques and defending in the rundown situation	Covering second and third base; running from second to third base; rundown practice

12	To defend home plate on balls hit to the infield	Covering home plate; fielding ground balls and throwing to home plate; running from third to home plate
13	To work on the hit-and-run	Hitting balls off the tee on the ground; attempting to run from first to third base; fielding and throwing to the proper base
14	To improve the mechanics of pitching	Throwing to each other; throwing to a catcher; throwing to a batter (working on control, velocity, and changing speeds on the pitch)

Season Plan for 12- to 14-Year-Olds

At this stage players are refining the skills they have learned from past years. This season plan builds on the previous one and adds a few new tactics, including stealing bases and holding runners on base.

Practice	Purpose	Tactics and skills
1	To evaluate players' overall playing abilities and identify their best positions	Pitching and hitting; throwing; catching; baserunning
2	To develop fielding and hitting techniques	Fielding grounders and fly balls; throwing to first base; hitting and running to first base
3	To teach rundowns, cutoffs, and baserunning strategies	Outfielders throwing balls to second and third base; baserunning; throwing balls to relay players and to bases
4	To work on stealing bases and offensive strategies	Taking the lead and sprinting from first to second base; hitting; practicing hit-and-run situations

5	To defend in the infield on force plays at second base	Running from first to second base; fielding grounders and throwing to second base for force plays
6	To work on pitching techniques and strategies	Pitching to a catcher; throwing to a batter; holding runners on base
7	To advance baserunners from second to third base	Bunting; baserunning; hitting behind the runner
8	To defend in the infield on tag plays at home plate	Covering home plate on tag plays; baserunning; bunts
9	To convert double plays from second base to first base	Double play pivots; relay and speed of the throw; baserunning
10	To work on offensive strategies, in particular the hit-and-run	Hitting behind the runner; advancing from first to third base
11	To defend on balls hit to the outfield with a runner on second base	Fielding in the outfield; backing up the outfielder; covering third base and home plate; cutoff throws; baserunning
12	To improve pitching techniques and strategies	Pitching (control, velocity); holding runners on base; hitting
13	To develop bat control, speed, and contact	Hitting off a batting tee; hitting against live pitching
14	To increase baserunning skills and strategies	Taking leads; advancing from first to third base; attempting to steal second base in a game situation; tagging up on third base on fly balls

Injury Report

Name of athlete _____

Date _____

Time _____

First aider (name) _____

Cause of injury _____

_____

Type of injury _____

Anatomical area involved _____

Extent of injury _____

_____

_____

First aid administered _____

_____

_____

Other treatment administered _____

_____

_____

_____

Referral action _____

_____

_____

_____

_____
First aider (signature)

Emergency Information Card

Athlete's name _____ Age _____

Address _____

Phone _____ S.S.# _____

Sport _____

List two persons to contact in case of emergency:

Parent or guardian's name _____

Address _____

Home phone _____ Work phone _____

Second person's name _____

Address _____

Home phone _____ Work phone _____

Relationship to athlete _____

Insurance co. _____ Policy # _____

Physician's name _____ Phone _____

IMPORTANT

Is your child allergic to any drugs? _____ If so, what? _____

Does your child have any other allergies? (e.g., bee stings, dust) _____

Does your child suffer from ____ asthma, ____ diabetes, or ____ epilepsy?

Is your child on any medication? _____ If so, what? _____

Does your child wear contacts? _____

Is there anything else we should know about your child's health or physical condition? If yes, please explain. _____

_____

_____

_____

_____

_____ _____

Signature   Date

Emergency Response Card

Information for Emergency Call
(be prepared to give this information to the EMS dispatcher)

1. Location _____

   Street address _____

   City or town _____

   Directions (cross streets, landmarks, etc.) _____

   _____

   _____

2. Telephone number from which the call is being made _____

3. Caller's name _____

4. What happened _____

   _____

   _____

   _____

   _____

   _____

5. How many persons injured _____

6. Condition of victim(s) _____

7. Help (first aid) being given _____

   _____

   _____

   _____

Note: Do not hang up first. Let the EMS dispatcher hang up first.

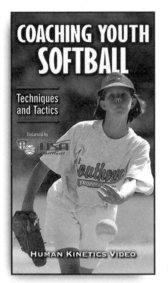